tasting along the wine road

cookbook

a collection of recipes from "A Wine & Food Affair"

cookbook **volume 11**

Recipes from the Wineries and Lodgings of the Alexander, Dry Creek and Russian River Valleys.

WINE ROAD
NORTHERN SONOMA COUNTY

A custom cookbook published by
Wine Road Northern Sonoma County
P.O. Box 46, Healdsburg, CA 95448

www.wineroad.com

Design © Pembroke Studios, www.pembrokestudios.com
Unless noted, photos © Lenny Siegel, www.siegelphotographic.com
Photo on Front Cover © Melody Mulligan
Photo on Back Cover © Caitlin McCaffrey
Photo of Truett Hurst Winery © Rob Scheid
Photo of Honor Mansion © Steve Aja

Thank you to the following members for submitting their photo:
Chalk Hill - DeLoach - Jenner Inn - Shelford House - Sonoma Orchid Inn

table of contents

table of contents

table of contents

foreword

executive chef Tom Schmidt
John Ash & Co., Santa Rosa, CA

My mother always cooked with fresh produce, and because I grew up in the Bay Area, I learned to appreciate the agricultural bounty Northern California has to offer. At age 14, I started my first garden, growing herbs, melons, pumpkins, tomatoes and carrots; I was so pleased to watch everything grow so quickly in the California sun.

Now that I've been a chef for 30 years, what better place to work than in Sonoma County, where I can feed my fascination with fresh foods and flavors, and take advantage of the vast variety of local produce, meats, seafood and wine available to restaurant and home cooks alike.

I lived for 20 years in northern Germany, where the sun rarely makes an appearance. I operated my own restaurant there, where fresh, local produce was limited. Now that I'm in warm, fertile Sonoma County, I have everything and more that I need in the way of ingredients, and the quality and freshness are incomparable.

Farmers markets give us access to ingredients produced in small quantities by quality-committed farmers. Heirloom vegetables, fantastic fruits, artisanal cheeses, complex baked breads, and myriad types of meats, poultry and sea-sweet treasures from the ocean are delivered right to our doors.

Sustainable farmstands such as Tierra Vegetables grow vegetables and fruits that are so fresh that they pop with flavor in your mouth. Grass-fed, hormone-free heritage chickens from Gleason Ranch are what chickens are supposed to be – firm of flesh and with real chicken flavor. Goat cheese from Bohemian Creamery reminds me of the best, soft French goat chevres. There is our famous Sonoma lamb, Petaluma duck, Dungeness crab, and the amazing bakers who honor old-world traditions.

And then there are the wines! Sonoma County wines are world-class, and come from prestigious appellations such as Alexander Valley, Chalk Hill, Dry Creek Valley, Russian River Valley and the Sonoma Coast. Take a drive around the county and you can see the different microclimates and soils that produce site-specific, distinctive Cabernet Sauvignons, Chardonnays, Pinot Noirs, Zinfandels and more, which I can pair with dishes made from fresh ingredients that are grown within a 30-mile radius of our restaurant.

At Vintners Inn and John Ash & Co., we have our own gardens, and I go out before each meal service to pick artichokes, figs, wild fennel, rhubarb, all types of thyme, mint, rosemary, basil, berries and other produce, which will become something delicious within a few hours.

As I returned from Europe, I dreamed of working and living in Sonoma County, and I cannot express how fortunate I feel to be here. I hope this cookbook provides you with a sense of the amazing bounty that Sonoma County offers, and the passionate people behind the food and wine.

recipes
from the wineries & lodgings

brunch

Applewood Inn & Restaurant

13555 highway 116, guerneville, ca 95446
707-869-9093

www.applewoodinn.com

Frittatas are a mainstay in Liguria in northern Italy, from which innkeeper Jim Caron's family hails. Frittatas are also a great way to use all the zucchini, Italian parsley and cherry tomatoes that come from the inn's organic garden, combined with one of the great goat cheeses made in Sonoma County. Here, we use Broncha from Achadinha Cheese Co. in Petaluma. **Serves 8**

brunch

Frittata

with zucchini & goat cheese

chef Jim Caron

ingredients

Frittata

10 eggs
1 teaspoon salt
2 tablespoons olive oil
2-3 small zucchini, sliced 1/8-inch thick
1 teaspoon dried oregano
2 tablespoons fresh Italian parsley, chopped
4 ounces Achadinha Broncha or other goat cheese, crumbled

Tomato-Arugula Salad

1 basket cherry tomatoes, halved
1 bunch arugula, stems removed
3 tablespoons olive oil
2 tablespoons fresh lemon juice
½ teaspoon salt
½ teaspoon ground black pepper

directions

For the frittata, whisk together in a bowl the eggs and ½ teaspoon of salt.

In a frying pan over medium heat, sauté the zucchini in the olive oil for about 2 minutes. Add the remaining ½ teaspoon salt, the oregano and half of the parsley. Sauté for another 2 minutes.

Add the eggs to the pan. Using a rubber spatula, quickly stir the eggs, lifting the cooked edges to allow the uncooked liquid to flow underneath. Evenly distribute the cheese on top of the eggs when they begin to firm up. Reduce the heat to low and cook 4 to 5 minutes more, without stirring.

If you are feeling brave, you can flip the frittata onto a flat lid and then slide the frittata back into the pan to finish cooking the other side, about 5 minutes more. If not, finish the top side of the frittata under a broiler. Using the spatula, gently loosen the edges from the pan and slide the frittata onto a serving plate. Garnish with the remaining parsley.

For the salad, combine the olive oil, lemon juice, salt and pepper in a small bowl. Toss the desired amount of dressing with the tomatoes and arugula leaves, and serve with the frittata.

Creekside Inn & Resort

16180 neeley road, guerneville, ca 95446
707-869-3623

www.creeksideinn.com

I serve these scones at breakfast and brunch, with scrambled eggs and crisp bacon, yet I think they would be just as good with soup or salad for lunch, or made smaller to accompany wine in the afternoon. An additional bonus: They can be made the night before. **Serves 12**

brunch

caramelized onion scones

with black pepper

chef Lynn Crescione

ingredients

½ cup butter
1 large sweet yellow onion, chopped
3 cups flour
3 tablespoons sugar
1-½ tablespoons baking powder
3 teaspoons ground black pepper
1 teaspoon salt
²/₃ cup half and half
2 eggs
melted butter for brushing the top

directions preheat oven to 400°

In a frying pan, melt the butter and sauté the onion until caramelized. Set aside to cool.

In a large bowl, mix the flour, sugar, baking powder, pepper and salt. Add the half and half, eggs and caramelized onions, and stir until just blended.

Knead the dough 6 times on a floured board. Place the dough on an ungreased baking sheet, and shape it into a circle about ½-inch thick. Cut the round into 12 wedges.

Bake for 12 to 15 minutes, then brush the scones with the melted butter, and allow them to cool to room temperature.

pair with a buttery sonoma county chardonnay

Farmhouse Inn & Restaurant

7871 river road, forestville, ca 95436
707-887-3300

www.farmhouseinn.com

In the winter, when Meyer lemons are in season, we serve these pancakes with a house-made lemon curd and a blood orange and Clementine compote. In summer, try them with fresh raspberries or blueberries and maple syrup. If serving with fresh berries, a little fresh thyme thrown into the batter is delicious. **Serves 2**

brunch

lemon-ricotta pancakes

chef Reyna Levaro

ingredients

¾ cup all-purpose flour
3 tablespoons sugar
1 tablespoon baking powder
¼ teaspoon salt
1 cup whole-milk ricotta (we use Bellwether Farms)
2 eggs
²/₃ cup whole milk
zest of 1 lemon (use Meyer lemons when in season)
juice of 1 lemon

directions

Sift together the flour, sugar, baking powder and salt. In a separate bowl, whisk together the ricotta, eggs, milk, lemon juice and lemon zest.

Add the dry ingredients to the wet and mix until combined.

Heat a cast-iron skillet over medium-high heat, and coat it with butter or oil. Drop ¼-cup batches of the batter into the skillet and cook until the edges look slightly dry, and bubbles form in the center; pancakes should be golden brown and slightly puffed. Serve with fresh, in-season fruit or maple syrup.

George Alexander House

423 matheson street, healdsburg, ca 95448
707-433-1358

www.georgealexanderhouse.com

This recipe is very simple, yet I am always asked for the recipe when I serve it to guests. The actual preparation time is under 10 minutes, though don't forget to thaw the spinach and allow the butter to soften in advance. Allow one hour for baking. **Serves 10**

brunch

eggs florentine

chef Holly Schatz

ingredients

1 10-ounce package frozen spinach, thawed and drained well
6 eggs, slightly beaten
½ pound sharp cheddar cheese, grated
1 quart small-curd cottage cheese
3 tablespoons flour
½ cup butter, softened

directions preheat oven to 350°

In a large bowl, combine all the ingredients. Pour the mixture into a 9- by 13-inch greased baking dish. Bake for 1 hour, or until the eggs have set. Cut into squares and serve.

pair with sauvignon blanc

Grape Leaf Inn

539 johnson street, healdsburg, ca 95448
707-433-8140

www.grapeleafinn.com

Although we serve this dish to our guests at breakfast,
it could easily be an entrée, with the addition of a fresh
spring greens salad and a chilled glass of white wine.
Look for garlic-chile sauce in Asian markets and the
ethnic foods aisle in supermarkets. **Serves 4**

smoked salmon paninis

with gruyere & chile-lime cream dipping sauce

ingredients

Chile-Lime Cream Dipping Sauce

¼ cup dry Sonoma County white wine
¼ cup fresh lime juice
1 tablespoon fresh ginger, peeled and chopped
1 tablespoon shallot, minced
⅓ cup whipping cream
2 tablespoons chili-garlic sauce
6 tablespoons (¾ stick) unsalted butter, room temperature, cut into ½-inch pieces

Paninis

8 large eggs
6 sprigs parsley, stems removed and chopped
6 sprigs cilantro, stems removed and chopped
6 sprigs dill weed, stems removed and chopped
6 chives, chopped
8 slices sourdough bread, ½- to ¾-inch thick, crusts cut off
8 ounces cream cheese, softened
2 cups Gruyere or Jarlsberg cheese, grated
¼ pound smoked salmon, thinly sliced

directions preheat panini grill to 515°; also preheat oven to 350°

For the dipping sauce, combine the first 4 ingredients in a small, heavy-bottomed saucepan. Boil over high heat until reduced by half, about 3 minutes. Add the cream and boil until reduced by half again, about 2 minutes. Reduce the heat to low, mix in the chili-garlic sauce, then add the butter, 1 piece at a time, whisking just until melted, before adding the next piece. Keep warm.

For the paninis, combine the eggs, parsley, cilantro, dill and chives in a bowl and whip into a batter.

Spread the 8 bread slices with a thin coating of softened cream cheese. Top 4 of the slices with ¼ cup of the Gruyere or Jarlsberg cheese, then cover the cheese of each sandwich with a ¼ portion of the sliced salmon. Top each of the 4 salmon-covered slices with another ¼ cup of cheese, and put the remaining 4 bread slices on top, forming 4 complete sandwiches.

Dip the sandwiches in the egg batter, making sure they are completely saturated. Lightly spray the panini press with Pam. Grill the sandwiches until they turn golden, which takes only a few minutes. Alternatively, fry them in a hot pan with melted butter until golden.

Using a spatula, remove the sandwiches to a tray that has been covered with a nonstick baking mat or parchment paper. Loosely cover the tray with foil and bake the sandwiches in the oven until the egg batter is cooked through, about 10 minutes. Cut the paninis on the diagonal and serve with Chili-Lime Cream Sauce.

Hope-Merrill House

21253 geyserville avenue, geyserville, ca 95441
707-857-3356

www.hope-inns.com

This cake is one of the few that actually improves with time. It can be prepared and stored for up to 3 days, and the lemon flavor will intensify during that time. **Serves 8**

brunch

meyer lemon
coffee cake

chef **Cosette Trautman-Scheiber**

ingredients

Streusel

1-¾ cups all-purpose flour
¾ cup packed light-brown sugar
1 teaspoon coarse salt
¾ cup cold unsalted butter

Glaze

1 cup confectioners' sugar, sifted
2 tablespoons Meyer lemon juice

Cake

5 Meyer lemons, cut into paper-thin slices, ends discarded
2 cups all-purpose flour
1 teaspoon baking powder
1 teaspoon baking soda
1-½ teaspoons coarse salt
½ cup unsalted butter, room temperature, plus more for pan
1 cup granulated sugar
3 tablespoons Meyer lemon zest (from 4 to 5 lemons), finely grated
2 large eggs
1 teaspoon pure vanilla extract
1 cup sour cream

directions preheat oven to 350°

To prepare the streusel, mix together the flour, brown sugar and salt. Using a pastry cutter or your fingers, cut the butter into the flour mixture, until small to medium clumps form. Cover and refrigerate until ready to use, up to 3 days.

To prepare the cake, cook the lemon slices in a medium saucepan of simmering water for 1 minute. Drain and repeat. Arrange the lemon slices in a single layer on a parchment-lined baking sheet.

Butter a 9-inch angel food cake pan. Sift together the flour, baking powder, baking soda and salt. In a large bowl, beat the butter, granulated sugar and lemon zest with a mixer on medium speed, until it's light and fluffy, about 2 minutes. With the mixer running, add the eggs, 1 at a time, then the vanilla. Reduce the speed to low and add the flour mixture in 3 additions, alternating with the sour cream.

Spoon half of the batter evenly into the cake pan. Arrange half of the lemon slices in a single layer over the batter. Spread the remaining batter evenly over the top. Cover with the remaining lemon slices in a single layer, then sprinkle the chilled streusel evenly over the batter.

Bake in the oven until the cake is golden brown, and a tester inserted in the center comes out clean, about 55 minutes. Transfer the pan to a wire rack set over a baking sheet, and let the cake cool in the pan for 15 minutes. Run a knife around the edges of the pan, and remove the outer ring. Let cool another 15 minutes, then run a knife around the center of the tube. Slide 2 wide spatulas between the bottom of the cake and the pan, and lift the cake to remove it from the center tube. Let cool completely on the rack.

Prepare the glaze just before serving the cake. Stir together the confectioners' sugar and lemon juice in a medium bowl. Drizzle the glaze over the cooled cake, letting the excess drip down the sides. Let the glaze set before slicing, about 5 minutes.

Inn at Occidental

3657 church street, occidental, ca 95465
707-874-1047

www.innatoccidental.com

While ready-made polenta is widely available in supermarkets and simple to prepare, the extra effort in making ground-corn polenta from scratch pays off handsomely in enhanced flavor and a luxurious texture. Polenta must be stirred often, to keep it from burning at the bottom of the pot. The elbow grease makes for a stirring dish! **Serves 8**

creamy polenta

with fruit compote

chefs Jerry & Tina Wolsborn

ingredients

Polenta

1 gallon water
½ pound butter
3-⅛ cups polenta
2 tablespoons salt
¼ pound Fontina cheese
¼ cup Parmesan cheese

Fruit Compote

1 cup apple juice
⅔ cup brown sugar
1 vanilla bean, cut lengthwise, seeds
scraped out and retained
1 cinnamon stick
5 allspice berries
½ teaspoon nutmeg
3 Granny Smith apples, cut into large dice
3 Bartlett pears, cut into large dice
¼ cup currants
1 Earl Grey tea bag
1 cup orange segments
½ cup grapefruit segments
1 cup maple syrup

directions

For the polenta, add the water and butter to a large stockpot and bring the mixture to a boil. Add the polenta slowly, stirring with a whisk, and stir until the polenta starts to get thick. Turn the heat to low and stir often, for 50 minutes. When the polenta is done, add the salt and cheeses, and keep the mixture warm in a double boiler.

For the fruit compote, add to a large stainless steel pot the apple juice, brown sugar, vanilla bean and seeds, and the spices. Simmer for 5 minutes, then add the apples, pears, currants and tea bag. Simmer for 8 minutes, or until the fruit is tender.

Strain the fruit, and reduce the remaining liquid over medium heat until it has a syrupy consistency. Remove the tea bag, add the liquid back to the fruit, then add the grapefruit and orange segments and maple syrup. Mix well, and serve over the warm polenta.

Old Crocker Inn

1126 old crocker inn road, cloverdale, ca 95425
707-894-4000

www.oldcrockerinn.com

Homemade scones are a staple of B & B's, and I enjoy making and serving them – from savory to sweet – with no added preservatives or artificial ingredients. A guest sent this recipe to us, and the first time I made these scones, they became instantly popular. They're sweet and don't really need butter or jam, though a little crème fraiche on the side is yummy. **Makes 19 scones**

white chocolate
pecan scones

chef Marcia Babb

ingredients

3 cups all-purpose flour
½ cup brown sugar
1 tablespoon baking powder
½ teaspoon baking soda
½ teaspoon salt
¾ cup unsalted butter, cut into small bits (handle as little as possible)
½ to ¾ cup dried cherries or cranberries, chopped
½ cup toasted pecans, chopped
1 cup white chocolate chips, or white chocolate block, chopped small
½ teaspoon vanilla extract
1 cup buttermilk

directions preheat oven to 400°

Place the flour, brown sugar, baking powder, baking soda and salt in the bowl of a food processor. Pulse until mixed. Add the butter and pulse just until the mixture resembles coarse cornmeal. Move the mixture to a large mixing bowl.

Mix the cherries, pecans and white chocolate chips in a small bowl, then stir them into the butter mixture.

Combine the vanilla and buttermilk, and add them to the dry ingredients, stirring with a fork just until moistened. Don't over-stir.

Turn the dough onto a lightly floured surface and knead just until it holds together, about 10 times. Cut the ball of dough into 2 smaller balls. Press the balls into circles about ½-inch thick. Cut them into uniform wedges, separate, and place them on a baking sheet covered with parchment paper. Repeat with the second ball.

Bake for 7 minutes, or until the scones are lightly browned.

The Raford House B & B Inn

10630 wohler road, healdsburg, ca 95448
707-887-9573

www.rafordinn.com

Who doesn't love scones? Our guests certainly do, and this recipe is one of their favorites. Even non-breakfast-eaters find themselves nibbling on these scones with their coffee or tea. **Serves 8**

brunch

orange toasted-almond
scones

chef Dana Pitcher and Rita Wells, Innkeepers

ingredients

Scones
2 cups all-purpose flour
1/3 cup sugar
2 teaspoons baking powder
pinch of salt
1/2 cup butter, chilled
2 eggs
1/4 cup orange juice
1 teaspoon vanilla extract
1 teaspoon orange zest
1/4 cup plus 1 tablespoon toasted, sliced almonds

Glaze
1 egg white mixed with 1/2 teaspoon water

directions preheat oven to 400°

In a large bowl or food processor, combine the flour, sugar, baking powder and salt. Cut the butter into 1/2-inch cubes, and blend them into the dry ingredients with a pastry blender or processor, until it resembles coarse crumbs.

In a small bowl, stir together the eggs, orange juice, vanilla and orange zest. Add this mixture to the dry ingredients and blend. Fold in 1/4 cup toasted almond slices.

With heavily floured hands, form the dough into a ball and put it onto a lightly floured surface. Roll the dough into an 8-inch diameter circle, and cut it into 8 pie-shaped wedges. Carefully place the wedges onto a parchment paper-lined baking sheet. Brush the tops with the egg glaze, sprinkle on the remaining toasted almonds, and bake for 20-25 minutes, until golden brown.

pair with sparkling wine or mimosas

Santa Nella House B & B

12130 highway 116, guerneville, ca 95446
707-869-9488

www.santanellahouse.com

Now that we raise our own chickens, we're always looking for ways to use our fresh eggs. Bob came up with this recipe, and he spices things up by serving his Mock Bloody Mary on the side, giving guests a complementary morning pick-me-up. **Serves 6**

brunch

enchiladas huevos

chef Bob Reeves and Betsy Taggart, Innkeepers

ingredients

Enchiladas Huevos

2 tablespoons butter
12 eggs
6 ounces ricotta cheese
6 green onions, chopped
1 8-ounce can enchilada sauce
8 ounces cheddar cheese, or half cheddar and half Monterey Jack, grated
6 flour tortillas
2 tablespoons cilantro, chopped

Mock Bloody Mary

6 ounces Clamato juice
1 teaspoon horseradish sauce
dash of salt, celery salt and black pepper
1 teaspoon lemon juice
dash of Worcestershire sauce
1-½ ounces Cahill Winery 24 Degree

directions preheat oven to 350°

To prepare the enchiladas, melt the butter in a 12-inch skillet. In a bowl, blend the eggs, ricotta and onions. Scramble the mixture in the warmed skillet, stirring gently until the eggs are creamy and set to desired consistency.

Coat a 16- by 10-inch baking pan with nonstick cooking spray. Spread a little of the enchilada sauce in the bottom of the pan.

In a separate dish, add most but not all of the enchilada sauce. Individually dip each tortilla into the sauce to coat both sides. Place the tortillas in the baking pan and fill them equally with the egg scramble. Roll the tortillas so that their seams rest on the bottom of the dish. Pour the remaining sauce over the top and sprinkle with the grated cheese. Bake for 20 minutes.

Sprinkle the chopped cilantro over the enchiladas and serve 1 per person. Avocado, sour cream, salsa, hot links and chorizo are optional additions.

For each Mock Bloody Mary, fill a cocktail shaker with ice. Add all the ingredients to the shaker, give it a 3-second shake, and pour into your favorite cocktail glass. Garnish with a celery stalk and a green olive, if desired.

Sonoma Orchid Inn

12850 river road, guerneville, ca 95446
707-887-1033

www.sonomaorchidinn.com

Innkeeper/chef Dana Murphy bakes this coffee cake in a decorative bundt pan, for a stylish presentation, though any tube pan will do. This is an exceptionally satisfying brunch offering, so decadent that it's also appropriate for a late-afternoon pick-me-up. **Serves 8**

sour cream
coffee cake

chef Dana Murphy

ingredients

Cake
12 tablespoons unsalted butter
1-½ cups sugar
3 large eggs
1-½ teaspoons vanilla
1-¼ cups sour cream
2-½ cups cake flour
2 teaspoons baking powder
½ teaspoon baking soda
½ teaspoon kosher salt

Streusel
¼ cup light brown sugar
½ cup all-purpose flour
1-½ teaspoons cinnamon
¼ teaspoon kosher salt
3 tablespoons cold unsalted butter
¾ cup walnuts, chopped

Glaze
½ cup confectioners' sugar
2 tablespoons maple syrup (not imitation)

directions preheat oven to 350°

For the cake, grease and flour a 10-inch tube pan. Cream the butter and sugar in the bowl of an electric mixer fitted with the paddle attachment, for 4 to 5 minutes. Add the eggs, 1 at a time, then add the vanilla and sour cream.

In a separate bowl, sift together the cake flour, baking powder, baking soda and salt. With the mixer set on low, add the flour mixture to the cake batter, until just combined. Finish stirring by hand with a spatula to ensure the batter is completely mixed.

For the streusel, place the brown sugar, flour, cinnamon, salt and butter in a bowl and pinch together with your fingers until it forms a crumble. Mix in the walnuts.

Set aside ¾ cup of the streusel. Sprinkle the rest in the tube pan. Spoon half the batter into the pan and spread it out with a knife. Sprinkle with ¾ cup streusel. Spoon the rest of the batter into the pan and spread it out with the knife. Lift the pan about 3 or 4 inches off the counter and let it drop so that the batter settles into the streusel topping. Bake for 50 to 60 minutes, until a cake tester comes out clean.

Let the cake cool on a wire rack for at least 30 minutes. Carefully transfer the cake onto a serving plate. For the glaze, whisk the confectioners' sugar and maple syrup together, adding a few drops of water if necessary, to make the glaze runny. Drizzle as much as you like over the cake, and serve.

appetizers

Arista Winery

7015 westside road, healdsburg, ca 95448
707-473-0606

www.aristawinery.com

Here is a wonderful way to prepare pork: slow-cooked with roasted peppers (my favorites are Jimmy Nardello's Italian frying peppers, yet even red bell peppers will do a great job). The pork drippings, wine and peppers create a beautiful sauce. **40 bite-sized portions**

appetizers

slow-cooked pork

with pinot noir & polenta

chef Bruce Riezenman, Park Avenue Catering

ingredients

Pork

4-5 pounds pork shoulder, boneless
1 red bell pepper, fire roasted on the grill and chopped
½ yellow onion, chopped
1 carrot, peeled and thinly sliced
1 cup Pinot Noir
6 garlic cloves, peeled and sliced
2 sprigs fresh rosemary
¼ cup olive oil
salt and pepper, to taste

Polenta

1 tablespoon butter
¼ yellow onion, minced
3 cups water
1 cup milk
1 cup instant polenta
½ cup Reggiano Parmesan cheese, grated
1 tablespoon extra virgin olive oil
2 tablespoons butter
kosher salt and white pepper, to taste

directions start the pork and polenta 1 day ahead of time

Ask your butcher to remove the bones from the pork shoulder and to tie (or "net") it as a roast.

To prepare the pork, combine all the ingredients and marinate the pork "open" overnight (if you are able to remove the net) by placing it in a baking dish. Turn it a few times during the day.

The next day, place the pork back in the net, or leave it "as is" if you've left it tied.

Preheat the oven to 250°. Place the pork with the marinade in a baking dish. Cover the pork and roast for 2 hours. Remove the cover and turn the temperature up to 300°, and continue to cook until the meat is very tender, about 1 hour. The liquid should be almost evaporated by then. If needed, add a small amount of water so the pork is not completely dry at the base. The pork should turn golden brown.

Remove the meat from the oven, allow it to cool, and pull the meat apart into chunks. Place the meat in a mixing bowl. Strain the pan drippings, pressing the vegetables through the strainer as much as possible. Remove the excess fat from the drippings, pour the drippings over the meat, and toss together. Cover and chill for use any time in the next few days.

To prepare the polenta, in a medium heavy-bottom pan, melt the butter over medium heat. Add the onion and sweat until it's soft but not brown.

Add the milk and water and bring to boil. Add a small amount of salt to give the water a very slight salty taste. Whisk in the polenta. Lower the heat and cook the polenta, stirring constantly with a wooden spoon, for 10-20 minutes, until the polenta is cooked. You can tell that by tasting; it should still have a bit of a firmness to the texture.

Remove the polenta from the heat and add the Parmesan cheese, olive oil and the rest of the butter. Season to taste with salt and white pepper.

Pour the polenta into a buttered baking dish, so that the mixture is ½- to ¾-inch high. Allow it to cool and place it in the refrigerator overnight to firm up. Cut the polenta into any shape you like, remove the shapes from the baking dish, and set them on a buttered or oiled baking sheet.

When ready to serve, place the polenta cakes in a hot oven, under the broiler or on the grill to warm and crisp their outsides. Place some warmed pork on a warm, crisp polenta cake, and drizzle with the pan juices.

pair with arista pinot noir

Branham Estate Wines

132 plaza street, healdsburg, ca 95448
707-473-0337
www.branhamestatewines.com

For 20 years, we have been going to the "Rockpile" to work and play – checking the vineyard, camping, cooking over an open fire, and always with a glass of wine. Our Campfire Gorgonzola Crostini is easy to make, and pairs well with friends, camping and wines made from the Rockpile appellation. **Serves 8**

campfire

gorgonzola crostini

chef Gary Branham

ingredients

1 bottle Branham Rockpile Zinfandel
5 ounces gorgonzola dulce cheese
2 ounces mascarpone
2 tablespoons walnut pieces, toasted
1 sourdough baguette

directions

Go camping. Start a campfire. Open a bottle of Branham Rockpile Zinfandel. Taste the wine.

Place a griddle on the campfire and heat it until it will burn your fingers.

Slice the baguette on the diagonal, about ½-inch thick, and toast the bread on the griddle until it's brown.

Mix the gorgonzola, mascarpone and walnuts in a bowl, and spread the mixture on the baguette slices while they're still warm. Enjoy while continuing to taste the wine.

pair with branham estate zinfandel

C. Donatiello Winery

4035 westside road, healdsburg, ca 95448
707-431-4442

www.cdonatiello.com

Chef Zoi Antonitsas describes her cooking as simple and rustic and, emphasizes the importance of using local, seasonal ingredients whenever possible. **Serves 8**

appetizers

chicken lettuce cups

chef Zoi Antonitsas, Zazu, Bovolo & Black Pig Meat Co.

ingredients

Chicken

2 tablespoons canola oil
1 tablespoon shallot, minced
1 teaspoon garlic, sliced
1 teaspoon fresh ginger, grated
1 pound chicken, ground
¼ cup soy sauce
2 tablespoons fish sauce
2 tablespoons sesame oil
2 tablespoons fresh cilantro, chopped
1 Fresno chile, minced
kosher salt, to taste
6 heads little gem lettuces, cleaned

Salad Topper

2 carrots, peeled and julienned
2 bunches scallions, sliced thin
1 red onion, julienned
1 English cucumber, julienned
½ cup rice wine vinegar
2 tablespoons fish sauce
2 tablespoons freshly-squeezed lime juice
1 Fresno chile, minced

directions

In a large sauté pan on medium heat, add the oil, shallots, garlic and ginger, and cook until the aromas are fragrant, about a minute.

Add the chicken and stir until it's cooked through, about 15 minutes.

In a large bowl, combine the chicken mixture with the soy sauce, fish sauce, sesame oil, cilantro and chile. Season to taste with salt.

In another bowl, toss the carrots, scallions, onion, cucumber, rice wine vinegar, fish sauce, lime juice and chile. Season to taste.

To assemble the lettuce cups, place the chicken in a lettuce leaf and top with the salad.

pair with c. donatiello chardonnay

Dutton Estate Winery

8757 green valley road, sebastopol, ca 95472
707-829-9463

www.duttonestate.com

A rich, savory mushroom filling is baked in flaky puff pastry to produce these irresistible hors d'oeuvres. For the best flavor, I like to use an all-butter frozen puff pastry, available at Whole Foods and other gourmet markets. To save time, the mushroom filling can be prepared a day ahead and kept refrigerated until time to assemble and bake. **Makes 18 Squares**

mushrooms in
puff pastry

chef Cynthia Newcomb

ingredients

3 tablespoons Cognac or brandy
½ cup heavy cream
2 tablespoons unsalted butter
2 or 3 shallots, sliced
¾ pound sliced mushrooms (trumpet, baby portobella, oyster, Chanterelle, shiitake, or a combination)
2 tablespoons fresh herbs (parsley, oregano, tarragon, basil or combination)
juice of ½ lemon
kosher salt and freshly ground pepper, to taste
1 sheet frozen puff pastry, thawed per package directions
¼ cup grated Gruyere cheese
1 egg white, slightly beaten

directions preheat oven to 450°

To prepare the filling, in a saucepan, add the Cognac or brandy and the cream, cook on low heat, and reduce by ⅓, stirring occasionally. Set aside.

In another pan, heat the 2 tablespoons of butter, add the shallots, and sauté until the shallots are soft. Add the mushrooms and continue cooking until the moisture is gone. Stir in the herbs and lemon juice, season with salt and pepper, then stir the brandy/cream mixture into the mushroom mixture. Adjust the seasoning if necessary.

To assemble, roll out the puff pastry on a lightly floured surface, to an 18- by 9-inch rectangle. Using a sharp knife or pizza cutter, cut the pastry into 3-inch squares, and place each square in the well of a muffin tin. Brush the interior bottoms of the squares with the egg white wash.

Put 1 heaping tablespoon of mushroom mixture in each pastry square and sprinkle with the cheese. Bake 12-15 minutes. Serve warm or at room temperature.

pair with dutton estate pinot noir

Everett Ridge Vineyards & Winery

435 west dry creek road, healdsburg, ca 95448
707-433-1637

www.everettridge.com

Chef Christoper Sterling has found that this recipe
is a favorite to both young and old at the winery's
club parties. The pork butt is marinated overnight,
so start this dish one day in advance. **Serves 15-17**

appetizers

pork nachos

chef Christopher Sterling

ingredients

3 cups water
2 cups Everett Ridge Diablita Blanca wine
¼ cup salt
⅓ cup light brown sugar
3 tablespoons Worcestershire sauce
4 tablespoons Everett & Jones Barbecue Sauce
2 tablespoons liquid smoke
1 boneless pork butt, approximately 8 pounds
tortilla chips, lightly salted
cheese of your choice, for grating

directions

To a 2-gallon re-sealable plastic bag, add the first 7 ingredients and mix well. Add the pork, seal the bag, and refrigerate the meat overnight, turning as often as possible.

Preheat the oven to 225°. Place the contents of the bag in a roasting pan, cover it with foil, and slow-cook the pork for 6 hours, or until the middle of the roast is 160°, measured by a meat thermometer.

Remove the pork from the pan— saving the cooking sauce — to a cutting board and shred it with 2 forks. Place the shredded meat back in the roasting pan with the cooking sauce.

Prepare a bed of tortilla chips, spoon the shredded pork and sauce onto the chips, and top with a light grating of cheese, then serve.

pair with everett ridge estate zinfandel

Fern Grove Cottages

16650 highway 116, guerneville, ca 95446
888-243-2674

www.ferngrove.com

(The appetizer comes with a bonus: in addition
to its savory deliciousness, it can be frozen,
uncooked, for up to a month. **Makes 26 bites**)

cheese & walnut bites

chef Margaret Kennett

ingredients

5 ounces Mexican cheese blend
4 ounces unsalted butter, softened
5 ounces all-purpose flour
pinch cayenne pepper
1 teaspoon paprika
1 tablespoon fresh thyme, chopped
pinch of salt
26 walnut halves
1 ounce Parmesan cheese, finely grated

directions preheat oven to 350°

In a large mixing bowl, beat the cheese and butter together. Gradually sift in the flour, spices, thyme and salt, and stir together into a soft dough.

Shape the dough into bite-size balls. Push a walnut half into the center of each ball and pinch the dough around the nut. Place the balls on a baking sheet, sprinkle them with the Parmesan cheese, and chill in the refrigerator for 30 minutes, until firm. Bake for 12-15 minutes, until golden brown, and serve warm.

pair with zinfandel

Haydon Street Inn

321 haydon street, healdsburg, ca 95448
707-433-5228

www.haydon.com

John Harasty (Haydon Street owner) was the executive chef at Churchill Downs in Louisville, KY for 12 years. During John's career, he has cooked for celebrity notables such as Ronald Reagan, George Bush, Burt Reynolds, Goldie Hawn, Rodney Dangerfield, Yule Brenner, Ozzy Osbourne, to name a few. **Serves 4 as an appetizer**

40

mushroom pizza

chef John Harasty

ingredients

Crust

1 package active dry yeast
1 cup warm water (105°-115°)
½ teaspoon salt
2 teaspoons olive oil
3-½ cups all-purpose flour
1 tablespoon cornmeal

Sauce

1 tablespoon all-purpose flour
2 tablespoons butter
1 cup half and half
½ teaspoon ground black pepper
dash of nutmeg
8 ounces brie cheese
¼ cup Romano cheese, shredded

Toppings

1 cup shredded mozzarella cheese
8-12 crimini mushrooms, sliced
fresh or dried tarragon, to taste
¼ cup Parmesan cheese, shredded

directions preheat oven to 500°

To prepare the pizza crust, dissolve the yeast in the warm water in a warmed bowl. Add the salt, olive oil and 2-½ cups of flour. Mix well. Add the remaining flour, mix, and turn out the dough on a floured surface, kneading into a ball.

Place the dough in a greased bowl in a warm place (no drafts). Cover the dough and let it rise until it doubles in size, about 1 hour. Punch down the dough.

Brush a 14-inch pizza pan with oil and sprinkle with the cornmeal. Press the dough across the bottom of the pan, forming a collar around the edge to hold the toppings. Use less dough for a thinner crust. Dough can be divided and refrigerated in a re-sealable bag for up to 1 week.

To prepare the sauce, in a saucepan, melt the butter and add the flour. Stir until they are completely blended. Add the half and half, black pepper and nutmeg, and cook over medium heat, stirring until the mixture boils. Add the brie and Romano cheeses, and continue stirring until it comes to a boil again. Adjust the thickness with more half and half, if necessary; it should have a pudding consistency.

To complete the pizza, cover the dough with the cheese sauce, then sprinkle evenly with the mozzarella cheese. Sprinkle on the sliced mushrooms and tarragon. Sprinkle the Parmesan across and bake for 10-12 minutes.

pair with chardonnay or pinot noir

Holdredge Winery

51 front street, healdsburg, ca 95448
707-431-1424

www.holdredge.com

We love using local ingredients and strongly recommend the Dry Creek Olive Oil Co. For this recipe, we use its "Three Orchards Blend" unfiltered extra virgin olive oil. **Serves 8 as an appetizer.**

wild mushroom tartlets

ingredients

8 4-inch tart shells
1 teaspoon butter
¼ small yellow onion, finely chopped
¼ pound crimini mushrooms, sliced
¼ pound Trumpet Royale (or other) wild mushrooms, chopped
salt and pepper, to taste
¼ cup Chardonnay
2 large eggs
2 cups heavy cream
Maldon salt, for finishing
extra virgin olive oil, for finishing

directions preheat oven to 350°

Place the tart shells on a baking sheet and bake in the oven until they turn light golden brown (15–20 minutes). Remove them from the oven, and keep the oven on.

In a medium sauté pan, heat the butter over medium heat. When the butter melts and begins to foam, add the onion and reduce the heat to low. Cover the pan and cook the mixture until the onions are soft and translucent.

Add the mushrooms, salt and pepper. Increase the heat to medium-high and sauté for 2 minutes, until the edges of the mushrooms begin to soften. Add the wine and cook uncovered, until all the liquid has evaporated. Reduce the heat toward the end of the cooking time to keep the mushrooms and the bottom of the pan from burning. Place the mushroom/onion mixture on a cutting board and chop slightly.

Meanwhile, place the eggs and cream in a mixing bowl. Whisk until they are well mixed. Add the warm chopped mushroom mixtures to the cream. Taste and add salt if needed.

Pour the mixture into the baked tart shells, until the filling is as high as you can go without the mixture spilling over. Make sure you have distributed all the mushrooms first, before topping them with the cream/egg mixture.

Bake the tartlets on a baking sheet for 20–25 minutes, until the centers of the tartlets are puffed and firm. Remove them and let them cool. When cool, cut the tartlets into quarters, sprinkle a few flakes of Maldon salt on the top, and add a few drops of olive oil. These can be served at room temperature, or reheated after they've been quartered.

pair with holdredge russian river valley pinot noir

Jordan Vineyard & Winery

1474 alexander valley road, healdsburg, ca 95448
707-431-5250

www.jordanwinery.com

While 12 savory cones may make for a fun Sunday project, 300 are our sous chef Manuel Reyes' worst nightmare on a bad day. Yet he's up to the task. You'll need 12 4-½-inch stainless steel cornet forms for this recipe. Feuille de brick is a dough used for light, crispy pastries. **Serves 12**

cornet of hamachi

& preserved lemon

ingredients

Cornets

2 sheets feuille de brick
canola spray
1 teaspoon Shichimi Togarashi (Japanese 7-spice)
1 egg white, lightly whipped

Hamachi

4 ounces ultra-fresh hamachi, finely diced
1 tablespoon white sesame seeds, lightly roasted
2 teaspoons green onions, minced
2 teaspoons preserved lemon or lemon zest,
finely minced
1 tablespoon Jordan extra virgin olive oil
2 tablespoons yuzu or Key lime juice
1 teaspoon toasted sesame oil
sea salt, to taste
daikon sprouts for garnish

directions preheat oven to 425°

Cut the brick sheets into 5-inch circles, then cut each circle in half. Spray the cornet forms with canola spray and set them aside on a rack.

Brush the brick semi circles with the egg whites, dust with Shichimi Togarashi spice, and wrap them about the cornet forms, Shichimi side up, to form cones. Bake the cones seam-side down until they are golden and crisp, 4-5 minutes. Carefully remove them from the forms and let them cool on a baking rack.

When the cones have cooled, combine all the hamachi ingredients at the last moment, except for the daikon sprouts, and adjust the seasoning. Top each cone with a heaping teaspoon of the hamachi and garnish with the sprouts.

pair with jordan chardonnay

Kendall-Jackson Wine Center

5007 fulton road, fulton, ca 95439
707-571-8100

www.kj.com

Arepas are traditional South American corn cakes that are filled with savory or sweet ingredients. This recipe makes appetizer-sized arepas filled with short ribs that are braised in a rich mole sauce. Mole can be purchased in jars and cans in Hispanic markets and some supermarkets. **Serves 12**

appetizers

braised short ribs arepas

chef Andrei Litvinenko

ingredients

2 cups masa harina
1 teaspoon baking powder
¼ teaspoon baking soda
1-½ teaspoons kosher salt
1 egg, beaten
2-½ cups warm water
¼ cup vegetable oil
1-½ tablespoons canned mole
¼ cup sour cream
2 cups braised short ribs, shredded
6 ounces shredded queso fresco cheese, shredded
1 bunch fresh cilantro leaves

directions preheat oven to 400°

Into a mixing bowl, sift the masa harina, baking powder, baking soda and salt. Mix thoroughly. Add the egg and mix. Add the water and mix. Let the batter sit for 10 minutes.

Heat a heavy skillet over medium high heat. Add the oil. Place ¼ cup of the batter into the pan and fry for 2 minutes on each side, until golden brown. Place the arepa onto a baking sheet. Repeat until all arepas are fried.

Place the baking sheet in the oven for 10 minutes. Remove the arepas from the oven and slice them in half, to make 2 rounds. In a bowl, combine the mole, sour cream and short ribs. Place the mixture onto the bottom half of each arepa round, top with 1 tablespoon of cheese and some cilantro leaves. Place the tops onto the arepas and serve.

pair with kendall-jackson highland estates hawkeye mountain cabernet sauvignon

La Crema Tasting Room

235 healdsburg avenue, healdsburg, ca 95448
707-431-9400

www.lacrema.com

We use local Fulton Valley Farms chickens in this smoked terrine. The smoke highlights Pinot Noir's complex toast and earth characteristics. The cranberry mostarda brings out the bright fruit aromas. Italian mostarda is made with preserved fruit, and gets its spiciness from powdered mustard seed. Sumac is available at Middle Eastern markets. **Makes 25-30 appetizers.**

appetizers

smoked chicken terrine

with cranberry mostarda

chef Eric Frishcorn

ingredients

Smoked Chicken Terrine

3 whole chickens
3 tablespoons sumac, ground
kosher salt, to taste
ground black pepper, to taste
2 cups chicken stock
1 cup parsley, chopped
1/8 cup thyme, chopped

Cranberry Mostarda

1 cup Pinot Noir
1 ounce Colman's Dry Mustard
4 tablespoons mustard seed
1-3/4 ounces shallots, minced
2-1/4 ounces butter
12 ounces fresh cranberries
4 ounces dried cranberries
1 cinnamon stick
1 tablespoon kosher salt
2 tablespoons red wine vinegar
5 tablespoons Dijon mustard
1/4 cup granulated sugar

directions prepare the terrine one day in advance

Preheat the oven to 350°. Season the chickens with sumac, salt and pepper, and smoke them for 1 hour.

In a roasting pan, cook the smoked chickens for 50 minutes in the oven. Remove them from the oven, leaving the juices in the pan, and allow the chickens to cool until they can be handled. Remove all the meat and shred it into a large bowl. Set aside.

Place the roasting pan onto medium heat and allow the juices to reduce until the pan is almost dry. Pour off the fat and discard. Deglaze the pan with the chicken stock and, on medium heat, reduce the liquid to 1/2 cup. Strain the reduced juices and pour them over the shredded chicken. Add the parsley and thyme, and season with salt and pepper. Line a 10- by 3- by 3-inch terrine mold with plastic wrap. Pack the chicken mixture into the mold and refrigerate overnight.

To prepare the mostarda, dissolve the dry mustard in the Pinot Noir. Add the mustard seeds, and let the mixture soak for at least 30 minutes.

Sauté the shallots in the butter, then add the fresh cranberries and continue cooking until they pop open. Add the rest of the ingredients and the mustard-Pinot Noir mixture, and simmer until slightly reduced, about 20 minutes. Cool slightly and blend in a food processor until the mixture is smooth.

To serve, carefully remove the chicken terrine from the mold. Slice it into 1/4-inch slices and serve with the mostarda.

pair with la crema russian river valley pinot noir

La Crema Winery

3690 laughlin road, windsor, ca 95492
707-571-1504

www.lacrema.com

For these flatbreads, we grill radicchio and combine it with Medjool dates to offset the slight bitterness of the radicchio; smoked mozzarella and fresh rosemary make each bite and sip of wine more exciting than the last. **Makes 6 pieces**

radicchio & medjool date

pizzetta with smoked mozzarella

chef Taki Laliotitis

ingredients

Dough

1-½ cups warm water
2 teaspoons dried yeast
4 cups high-gluten flour plus ¼ cup for flouring
2 tablespoons kosher salt

Pizzetta

¼ cup extra virgin olive oil
1-½ cup scarmoza (smoked mozzarella), grated

Radicchio & Medjool Mix

2 garlic cloves, minced
¼ teaspoon rosemary, minced
¼ teaspoon thyme, mixed
2 tablespoons balsamic vinegar
2 tablespoons vegetable oil
2 heads radicchio, each quartered
1 cup Medjool dates, pitted
¼ cup balsamic vinegar
salt and pepper, to taste

directions preheat grill to 500°; preheat oven to 475°

To prepare the dough, mix the water and yeast in a mixing bowl. Add the flour, then the salt, keeping the ingredients separate. Do not mix. Allow the yeast to activate and create bubbles.

When you see this, mix the dough in an electric mixer, using a dough hook attachment. Mix until well incorporated, about 5-8 minutes. If the dough is wet, add flour until the dough pulls away from the side of bowl. Cover the bowl with plastic wrap and allow it to rise until it doubles in size. Punch down the dough and divide it into 4 equal balls. Cover the dough and allow it to rise for another 20-30 minutes.

To prepare the radicchio, heat a grill to medium-high. Place the garlic, rosemary, thyme, 2 tablespoons of balsamic vinegar, oil and quartered radicchio in a large bowl. Season with salt and pepper, and toss together. Let rest for 5 minutes.

Grill the radicchio well on all sides, then place them on a cutting board. Remove the core of the radicchio so that the leaves fall apart. Rough-chop the leaves and place them into a bowl.

Quarter the dates and mix with the second portion of vinegar to prevent the dates from sticking. Pour the mixture into a 12-inch sauté pan. Bring the mixture to a simmer, and add the radicchio. Cook until the vinegar has almost gone dry, remove the pan from the heat, and chill the mixture immediately. Season with salt and pepper.

When the dough has rested, flour a work surface and roll out a ball of dough to 12-14 inches in diameter. Shake off the excess flour and place the dough in a baking pan. Brush the dough with extra virgin olive oil. Spread the radicchio/date mixture over the dough. Lightly cover with the smoked mozzarella and bake the pizzetta in the oven for 6-8 minutes. Remove the pan from the oven and cut the pizzetta into 6 pieces.

pair with la crema pinot noir

Marimar Estate Vineyards & Winery

11400 graton road, sebastopol, ca 95472
707-823-4365

www.marimarestate.com

Romesco is a quintessential Catalan sauce, indigenous to the city of Tarragona. Every cook has a different way of making it; this is my favorite of a half-dozen you'll find in my cookbook, "The Catalan Country Kitchen," because it uses ingredients easily available here. I accompany the sauce with the small meatballs we call pilotas in Catalonia. **Serves 8**

marimar's romesco sauce
with pilotas (catalan meatballs)
chef Marimar Torres

ingredients

Romesco Sauce
1 tablespoon olive oil for frying
1 large (½-inch-thick) slice of white bread
½ cup whole almonds, toasted
¼ teaspoon hot red pepper flakes
1 large garlic clove, coarsely chopped
½ cup roasted red bell peppers or pimientos from a jar
(preferably fire-roasted, from Spain)
½ pound ripe tomatoes
¼ teaspoon paprika
¼ teaspoon salt, or to taste
½ teaspoon freshly ground black pepper, or to taste
¼ cup red wine vinegar
½ cup extra virgin olive oil

Pilotas
1 pound medium-ground pork
1 cup homemade bread crumbs
(crusts removed)
2 eggs, beaten
3 tablespoons fresh parsley leaves, chopped
3 large garlic cloves, minced
¼ cup pine nuts
½ teaspoon salt
½ teaspoon ground black pepper
⅛ teaspoon ground cinnamon
1 tablespoon olive oil for sautéing

directions

For the sauce, heat the 1 tablespoon of oil in a small skillet, and over medium heat, fry the bread slice until it's golden on both sides. Grind the toasted almonds finely in a food processor, together with the bread, pepper flakes and garlic. Add the red peppers, tomatoes, paprika, salt and pepper, and purée to form a smooth paste. Whirl in the vinegar, and with processor running, add the ½ cup of olive oil slowly, in a thin stream. Taste and adjust the seasoning, if necessary.

To prepare the pilotas, mix all the ingredients except for the olive oil in a large bowl. With your hands, make small meatballs the size of a nickel. In a small skillet, heat the oil over medium heat, and sauté the meatballs in small batches until they're cooked through. Serve with the Romesco sauce.

pair with marimar estate don miguel chardonnay and pinot noir

Martin Ray Winery

2191 laguna road, santa rosa, ca 95401
707-823-2404

www.martinraywinery.com

This recipe is easy and fun to eat. The combination of the caramelized onions and blue cheese pair well with Merlot. Use a good sharp blue, such as local Point Reyes Farmstead Blue, and excellent quality grass-fed beef. The Merlot-onion recipe makes more than you need for the burgers. It will keep in the fridge for two weeks and is great, served warm or cold, on sandwiches, grilled chicken and steaks. **Serves 8**

slider burgers

with merlot-caramelized onions & blue cheese

chef Bruce Riezenman, Park Avenue Catering

ingredients

Merlot-Caramelized Onions

4 medium red onions, peeled and thinly sliced
2 cups Merlot
½ cup sugar
2 tablespoons balsamic vinegar
2 bay leaves
pinch salt
pinch cayenne

Sliders

1-½ pounds ground beef (18-20% fat)
kosher salt, to taste
fresh ground black pepper
1 teaspoon rosemary, chopped
8 small rolls (potato rolls or any other that is soft and small)
¼ pound blue cheese
1 cup Merlot-Caramelized Onions

directions

To prepare the onions, place all the ingredients in a heavy bottomed sauce pot. Turn the heat to high, cover tightly and simmer for 15 minutes. Lower the heat to medium-high, remove the cover and continue cooking for about 45 minutes, stirring occasionally.

As the liquid starts to thicken, lower the heat and stir with a wooden spoon until it is almost all evaporated. Allow the mixture to cool. Taste and add salt if needed. Store in a glass jar in the refrigerator.

To prepare the sliders, pre-heat a grill to medium-hot.

Form the ground beef into small patties, approximately 2-½ to 3 ounces each. Be careful to press them gently so they remain tender. Sprinkle both sides of the patties with salt, ground pepper and rosemary. Rub a little oil on the pre-heated grill and cook the burgers to medium-rare.

While the sliders are cooking, split the buns in half and toast them on the corner of the grill. Place 1 cooked burger on each bun bottom. Top with blue cheese, followed by warm caramelized onions.

pair with martin ray or angeline merlot

Mazzocco Sonoma Winery

1400 lytton springs road, healdsburg, ca 95448
707-431-8159

www.mazzocco.com

While we often serve these meatballs as an appetizer,
they can also be combined with pasta or rice as a
main course. **Serves 12 as an appetizer**

lamb & rosemary meatballs

with tomato rice pilaf & blackberry gastrique

chef Ryan Waldron

ingredients

Lamb Meatballs

1 pound fresh ground lamb
1-½ tablespoons fresh rosemary, finely chopped
1 medium shallot, diced
½ tablespoon kosher salt
½ tablespoon cracked pepper
1-½ teaspoons marjoram
2 teaspoons golden balsamic vinegar
½ cup fresh breadcrumbs
salt and black pepper, to taste

Blackberry Gastrique

5 cups fresh blackberries
1-½ cups sugar
1 cup golden balsamic or rice wine vinegar

Tomato Rice Pilaf

2 cups chicken or vegetable stock
2 teaspoons olive oil
1 cup long-grain white rice
½ cup green onions, chopped
½ cup celery, chopped
1 tomato, flash steamed, skin removed, medium-chopped
¼ bunch fresh parsley, coarsely chopped
salt and white pepper, to taste

directions preheat oven to 400°

To prepare the meatballs, add all the ingredients to a large bowl, and using your hands, completely mix together. Cover the bowl with plastic wrap and let sit for about an hour.

Roll out all the meat into balls slightly larger than golf balls. Bake them for approximately 15 minutes, or until done.

To prepare the pilaf, place the stock in a large saucepan and heat it on the stovetop. Keep the stock hot while preparing the rice.

In a large skillet, heat the olive oil over medium-high heat. Add the rice to the skillet and brown the grains, stirring constantly for 2-3 minutes. Add the chopped onion and celery, and continue to stir until the onions/celery begin to soften, about 1-2 minutes.

Carefully add the rice mixture to the stock. Bring the mixture to a simmer, and lower the temperature. Cover the pot and cook the rice for 15-20 minutes, without removing the cover during cooking. After the rice is cooked, remove the cover and let the rice sit. Add the chopped tomato, parsley, salt and pepper, and gently stir with a fork to fluff the rice.

To prepare the gastrique, in a saucepan, mash the blackberries with the back of a spoon. Add the sugar and vinegar, bring the liquid to a boil, and reduce the heat to a simmer. Cook the mixture for 25-30 minutes, or until it becomes thick and syrupy. Remove it from the heat and strain through a fine-mesh sieve.

To assemble the appetizer, place a small amount of the rice onto a small plate or in a small soufflé cup. Place 1 or 2 meatballs on top of the rice, and using a spoon, drizzle the gastrique over the meat.

pair with mazzocco zinfandel

Murphy-Goode

20 matheson street, healdsburg, ca 95448
707-431-7644

www.murphygoodewinery.com

For our version of kefta, a ground meat kabob, we combine the spices of the Middle East with fresh herbs to season the lamb. A glaze of pomegranate molasses, which can be purchased in Mediterranean and Asian markets, makes this pairing a "Jackpot" with our Zinfandel. **Makes 25, 1-ounce portions**

appetizers

lamb keftas

with pomegranate molasses glaze

chef Andrei Litvinenko

ingredients

25 8-inch bamboo skewers
1 pound ground lamb
5 ounces ground pork fat
1 teaspoon ground black pepper
½ cup yellow onion, minced
1 tablespoon garlic, minced fine
1 tablespoon fresh mint, minced fine
½ cup fresh parsley, minced fine
1 teaspoon fresh rosemary, minced fine
½ teaspoon cayenne pepper
½ teaspoon cumin
½ teaspoon nutmeg, fresh ground
½ teaspoon cinnamon
3 tablespoons kosher salt
¼ cup pomegranate molasses

directions

Soak the bamboo skewers in water for 1 hour.

In a large bowl, combine all the ingredients except the skewers and pomegranate molasses. Mix thoroughly and divide into 25 portions. Take each portion and form it into a 3-inch-long "sausage" on each of the skewers. Refregerate until ready to grill.

Place the pomegranate molasses in a small saucepan over low heat, and warm it slowly until it reduces to thick and syrupy. Remove the molasses from the heat and reserve.

Grill the kefta skewers to medium-rare. Brush them with the pomegranate glaze and serve immediately.

pair with murphy-goode jackpot zinfandel

Rued Vineyards & Winery

3850 dry creek road, healdsburg, ca 95448
707-433-3261

www.ruedvineyards.com

The Rued Family started a tradition of farming and grape growing in 1882 in Sonoma County. We have now started a new tradition of making wine. Please come, meet our family and taste our wine. **Makes 24 biscotti**

appetizers

parmesan

black pepper biscotti

chef Tracy Bidia, T & Company / A Private Affair Catering

ingredients

4 cups all-purpose flour, plus additional for dusting
2 teaspoons baking powder
1-½ teaspoons kosher salt
1-½ tablespoons fresh black pepper
2-½ ounces Parmigiano-Reggiano cheese, finely grated
1-½ sticks cold salted butter, cut into ½-inch cubes
4 eggs
1 cup whole milk

directions preheat oven to 350°

In a large bowl, whisk together the flour, baking powder, salt, 1 tablespoon of black pepper and 2 cups of the cheese. Blend in the butter with a pastry blender or a fork, until the mixture resembles course cornmeal.

In another bowl, whisk 3 of the eggs with the milk and add to the flour mixture, stirring with a fork until a soft dough forms.

Turn the dough out onto a lightly floured surface and divide into quarters. Using well-floured hands, form each piece into a slightly flattened, 12-inch-long log (2 inches wide by ¾-inch high). Transfer the logs to 2 ungreased large baking sheets, arranging the logs about 3 inches apart.

Whisk the remaining egg and brush over the logs. Sprinkle the tops of the logs evenly with the remaining cheese and pepper. Bake the biscotti, rotating and switching position of the sheets halfway through baking, until the logs are pale golden and firm, about 30 minutes. Let the logs cool for about 10 minutes.

Reduce the oven temperature to 300°. Carefully transfer the loaves to a cutting board and with a serrated knife, cut them diagonally into ½-inch-thick slices. Arrange the slices, cut side down, in 1 layer on a baking sheet. Repeat with the remaining logs

Bake the biscotti again, turning over once, until they are golden and crisp, 35 to 45 minutes. Cool them for 15 minutes before serving.

pair with rued zinfandel

Russian River Vineyards

5700 gravenstein highway north, forestville, ca 95436
707-887-3344

www.russianrivervineyards.com

Ever mindful of its treasured past, the new owners of Russian River Vineyards are meticulously renovating the estate, with the goal of transforming it into a modern-day archetype of an organic, sustainable and "green" winery. **Serves 10**

peppered rare ahi tuna

with grilled asparagus

chef Gregory Hallihan

ingredients

1 small handful peppercorns
1 pound high-grade ahi tuna loin
2 tablespoons olive oil
1 pound asparagus, tough ends snapped off
2 tablespoons truffle oil
1 cup sour cream
2 tablespoons prepared horseradish
3 tablespoons soy sauce

directions

Crush the peppercorns as finely as possible; a coffee grinder works well. Roll the ahi loin lightly in the peppercorns.

Add 1 tablespoon of the olive oil to a sauté pan and heat it on high. Add the ahi loin to the pan and quickly sear it on all sides, turning every 15 seconds. You want the exterior seared, and the center still rare.

Lightly toss the asparagus in the remaining 1 tablespoon of olive oil and grill or broil it until it's cooked through yet still tender.

In a small bowl, whisk the sour cream and horseradish together.

To assemble, cut the ahi and asparagus into bite-size pieces. On a serving plate, place the tuna and asparagus in alternating layers. Drop the horseradish cream around and on the ahi and asparagus, and drizzle them with the truffle oil and soy sauce. Serve immediately.

pair with russian river vineyards sauvignon blanc or pinot noir

Sapphire Hill Winery

55 front street, healdsburg, ca 95448
707-431-1888

www.sapphirehill.com

When our daughter, Hannah, was a toddler, she was fussy about what she ate. One evening, we were enjoying this pâté and offered Hannah a bite. She ever-so-reluctantly tasted it and, to our surprise, wanted more. We couldn't feed her fast enough. 'More pate, Daddy!' became her mantra. This recipe is best with lamb bacon rashers, which must be prepared 5 days in advance (see recipe). Good-quality bacon is a suitable substitute. **Serves 5-6**

appetizers

terrine de campagne d'agneau
(country lamb pâté)

chef Anne Giere

ingredients

2 tablespoons butter plus more to grease terrine
1 medium onion, finely diced
3 cloves garlic, finely diced
11 ounces lamb belly, cut into small dice (or ground lamb)
6 ounces lamb back fat, cut into small dice (if you can't get lamb fat, increase the portion of lamb meat by 6 ounces)
2 teaspoons salt
½ teaspoon pepper
1-½ teaspoons parsley
1-½ teaspoons thyme
1 teaspoon 4-spice mixture (1 ounce each of fine-ground black pepper, cinnamon and nutmeg, and ½ ounce ground clove)
4 ounces chicken liver, cleaned
2 ounces pistachios
2 eggs
lamb bacon rashers, sliced thin, or regular bacon

directions preheat oven to 325°

To prepare the pâté, heat the butter in a sauté pan, add the onions and garlic, sweat the vegetables, then let them cool. Add the onions and garlic to the bowl of a food processor and blend.

In a meat grinder, grind the lamb belly and back fat and place them in a large bowl. Add the onion/garlic mixture, salt, pepper, parsley, thyme and 4-spice, and mix well. With a rubber spatula, fold in the chicken liver, pistachios and eggs.

Line a 10- by 3-inch terrine with butter. Add a layer of plastic wrap, with enough overlap to fold the excess completely over the terrine, after the terrine has been filled. On top of the plastic wrap, add the bacon of your choice. Fill the terrine ¾-full with the pâté mixture, and fold the bacon over the pâté. If necessary, cover any exposed pâté with more bacon before folding the ends over to seal it.

Then fold the excess plastic wrap over the terrine, sealing it completely. Cover with the terrine lid or aluminum foil, and place it in 6-inch-deep hotel pan. Fill the pan with hot water ²/₃ of the way up the outside of the terrine. Put the pan in the oven and bake until the internal temperature of the pâté reaches 139 degrees on a meat thermometer.

Let the terrine cool for 15 minutes, then press the pâté tightly into the terrine mold, with 25 pounds of pressure, overnight in the refrigerator. The next day, serve 2-3 slices per person on a small bed of frisée greens.

Lamb Bacon Rashers (make 5 days ahead)
Mix thoroughly 1 cup salt with 2 cups brown sugar. Rub the lamb belly with the mixture, covering the meat completely. Place the meat in a large re-sealable bag, seal it and lay the bag flat in the refrigerator. Leave the meat alone to cure for 2 days, then flip over the bag, lay flat again, and allow to cure for 3 more days. You will see a liquid build up in the bags; leave it there. After 5 days, remove the bacon from the bag, dry well with paper towels and cut into thin bacon strips.

pair with sapphire hill estate pinot noir or syrah

Stephen & Walker Winery

243 healdsburg avenue, healdsburg, ca 95448
707-431-8749

www.trustwine.com

This recipe is ultra-easy and sumptuous. The amount of anchovy fillets, garlic and capers can be increased, according to your taste. Everyone loves this spread and will want your recipe! **Serves 4**

tapenade

(olive spread)

chef Nancy Walker

ingredients

2 cups kalamata olives, pitted
3 anchovy fillets
1 clove garlic, finely ground into paste
2 teaspoons capers
4-6 tablespoons olive oil

directions

In the bowl of a food processor, place all the ingredients. Finely chop them, and with the blades running, slowly add the olive oil, making a smooth and spreadable paste.

Refrigerate the paste overnight for the best flavor, and serve at room temperature. Spread the tapenade on your favorite bread, toast, bagel or crackers.

pair with stephen & walker sauvignon blanc

Taft Street Winery

2030 barlow lane, sebastopol, ca 95472
707-823-2049

www.taftstreetwinery.com

A fun way to serve these spicy treats is to make a single long sausage, making sure it is not too tightly packed. Then roll the sausage into a single spiral. Put a skewer or two through the sausage to keep it intact, and cut off pieces as needed. **Serves 8-10**

sausage
taft street style

ingredients

2 pounds lean pork
1 pound lean beef
1 pound pork back fat
1 cup Matos St. George cheese
1 cup Taft Street Dry Creek Valley Syrah St. Emydius Acre
¼ cup Italian parsley, chopped
1 tablespoon freshly ground pepper
1 tablespoon ground fennel seeds
1 tablespoon garlic, chopped
1 tablespoon salt
1 tablespoon red pepper flakes
hog casings

directions preheat a grill

In a large bowl, combine the meats, back fat and cheese. Grind or coarsely chop the mixture. Combine the remaining ingredients and add them to the meat mixture, kneading it thoroughly.

Stuff the mixture into one long hog casing, or several shorter ones. Grill the sausages until done. Alternatively, cook them in a smoker for a different flavor.

pair with taft street dry creek valley syrah st. emmydius acre

Trentadue Winery

19170 geyserville avenue, geyserville, ca 95441
707-433-3104

www.trentadue.com

This is a red-wine-friendly dish that can be made with a bit of extra stew left over from the night before. When we make these risotto balls for guests, we braise short ribs with the red wine we are pairing them with, although you can use any braised beef, pork or lamb. **Makes 32 appetizers**

appetizers

risotto balls

(arancini with braised short ribs)

ingredients

Risotto

2 tablespoons salted butter
¼ cup yellow onion, diced
salt and pepper, to taste
1 cup arborio rice
2 bay leaves
¼ teaspoon fresh thyme, chopped
1 quart chicken broth, hot
⅓ cup Parmesan cheese, grated
1 large egg, beaten

Arancini

Braised short ribs, pork or beef, chilled and cut into
32 small, ⅜-inch cubes
3 cups dried, coarse breadcrumbs
3 cups canola oil
¼ cup balsamic glaze or aged balsamic vinegar

directions

To prepare the risotto, place the butter and onions in a small sauce pot over medium heat. Add the salt and pepper. Cover and cook for 5 minutes, until the onions are soft. Add the rice, bay leaves and thyme. Cover and cook for 3 minutes.

Add the hot chicken broth, 1 cup at a time, and gently stir until almost all the liquid has been absorbed, then add the next cup of broth. When you are done (25-30 minutes), the rice should be plump and cooked with a very slight "bite." Remove it from the heat and gently stir in the Parmesan. Cool to room temperature, then stir in the egg.

To make the arancini, scoop 2 tablespoons of risotto into your hand and make an impression with your thumb, deep and wide enough to hold the meat. Put a dab of braising sauce on the meat and enclose it with the risotto. Form the meat-studded rice into a sphere the size of a golf ball, rolling it in your hand to make it as round as possible. Coat it generously with dried breadcrumbs. Repeat with the remaining risotto.

Preheat the canola oil and fry the arancini on all sides, until they're golden brown. Drizzle them with balsamic glaze and serve.

pair with trentadue la storia cuvee 32

Vintners Inn

4350 barnes road, santa rosa, ca 95403
800-421-2584

www.vintnersinn.com

I often prepared this dish when I cooked in Europe, using sardines from southern Spain. Fresh sardines from Monterey Bay are just as delicious, and the addition of a sauce made from local tomatoes and basil makes it a light, bright appetizer for late summer and fall. **Serves 4**

marinated sardines

with tomato basil sauce on a parmesan cookie

chef Tom Schmidt

ingredients

Sardines

12 fresh Monterey Bay sardines (not too large)
¼ cup coarse sea salt
½ cup extra virgin olive oil

Tomato Basil Sauce

1 yellow onion
$1/3$ cup extra virgin olive oil
8 ripe tomatoes
¼ cup red wine vinegar
salt and pepper, to taste
1 bunch basil, stems removed
piment d' Espelette (dried red pepper)
Thai fish sauce

Parmesan Cookies

4 ounces Parmesan cheese, finely grated
4 ounces all-purpose flour
4 ounces butter, softened

directions

Scale and filet the sardines. Place them skin-side down on a towel and sprinkle them with the sea salt. Cover the sardines with plastic wrap and put them in the refrigerator for 4 hours. Rinse them with cold-running water and pat them dry. Cover with the olive oil.

To prepare the tomato sauce, peel and mince the onion, and sauté it slowly with the olive oil until the onion is translucent. Blanch the tomatoes, then seed and cut them into coarse chunks, reserving the seeds and juice. Add the tomatoes to the onions and simmer the mixture for about 30 minutes. Add the vinegar, salt and pepper, and slowly reduce the mixture until it's thick. Refrigerate.

Julienne ¾ of the basil leaves and mix them into the chilled tomato sauce. Put the reserved tomato seeds and juice in a fine strainer and reduce the juice to ¼ its original volume. Put the juice into a small container and, with an immersion blender, mix in the olive oil until it emulsifies. Adjust the seasoning with Thai fish sauce and piment d'Espelette.

To make the cookies, knead the Parmesan, flour and butter together, just until the dough comes together (don't overwork it). Wrap the dough in plastic wrap and chill for an hour.

Roll out the chilled dough to ¼-inch thick and cut it into 2- by 5- by 4-inch rectangles. Bake the dough in a preheated 375° oven for approximately 10 minutes. Allow to cool.

To finish, put the cookies on plates and smear on 1 heaping tablespoon of the tomato basil sauce on each. Remove the sardines from the oil and pat them dry with paper towels. Place 4 sardine filets next to each other on each cookie. Julienne the rest of the basil leaves and scatter them on the sardines. Decorate the plate with the tomato syrup and serve.

pair with ferrari-carano fume blanc

Wilson Winery

1960 dry creek road, healdsburg, ca 95448
707-433-4355

www.wilsonwinery.com

In 2001, we opened a tasting room on the backside of the old barn. When you think "backside of the barn", you don't picture a breathtaking panoramic view of Dry Creek Valley. But that is what you will find behind this barn. As you relax on the tasting room veranda, it is easy to lose track of time as you soak in one of the finest views of the valley while sipping a glass of Wilson wine...enjoying quesadillas and our now-famous tri tip! **Serves 8**

caramelized onion quesadillas

with roasted red pepper and tomato basil salsa

chef Diane Wilson

ingredients

Tomato Basil Salsa

3 ripe tomatoes, seeded and diced
¼ cup red onion, chopped
2 garlic cloves, minced
1 jalapeno pepper, finely chopped (optional)
2 tablespoons olive oil
¼ cup fresh basil, chopped
salt and pepper, to taste

Quesadillas

2 tablespoons olive oil
2 sweet yellow onions, halved and thinly sliced
2 tablespoons balsamic vinegar
2 red peppers, roasted (or 1 jar roasted red peppers)
1 tablespoon vegetable oil
¾ cup grated sharp white Cheddar cheese
¾ cup grated Monterey Jack cheese
3 tablespoons fresh basil, chopped
8 flour tortillas
sour cream (optional)

directions preheat oven to 500°

To prepare the salsa, toss all ingredients together in a mixing bowl, and season with salt and fresh ground pepper to taste. Set aside.

To prepare the quesadillas, first caramelize the onions. Heat the oil in a medium sauté pan over medium heat. Add the onions and cook until they're soft and caramelized, stirring regularly, about 30-40 minutes. Add the balsamic vinegar and cook about 5 minutes more, until the liquid has evaporated.

To roast the red peppers, rub them with vegetable oil and place them on a foil-covered baking sheet. Roast in the oven until the peppers are blistered and blackened. Place them in a glass bowl and cover with plastic wrap for 10 minutes. Peel, seed and cut the peppers into thin strips. Reduce oven heat to 425°.

To assemble the quesadillas, place 4 tortillas on a work surface. Divide, in order, among the 4 tortillas the 2 cheeses, caramelized onions, roasted peppers and the basil. Top with the remaining 4 tortillas, brush the tops with oil, and transfer to a baking sheet. Cook for 8-10 minutes, until the cheese is melted and the tortilla tops golden brown. Cut the quesadillas into quarters and serve with the tomato basil salsa and sour cream.

Windsor Oaks Vineyards & Winery

10810 hillview road, windsor, ca 95492
707-433-4050

www.windsoroaks.com

Being born into a Greek family, we learned how to entertain and cook at a very young age. This dish is a wonderful finger food at cocktail parties and can be used as the main course for lunch or dinner poolside. For an added touch, top the meat with tzatziki, a Greek yogurt, cucumber and dill dip found in the deli section of most grocery stores. Opa! (That's "cheers" in Greek). **Serves 10-12**

appetizers

shaved greek lamb

with garlicky white bean hummus on toasted pita chips

chef Regina Novello

ingredients

Lamb

6 garlic cloves, crushed
¼ cup chopped fresh rosemary
¼ cup chopped fresh oregano
¼ cup olive oil
juice from 1 lemon
1 teaspoon salt
1 tablespoon ground pepper
4-5 pounds butterflied or leg of lamb

White Bean Hummus

2 14-ounce cans cannellini beans, drained,
with juice reserved
½ cup garlic cloves, roasted
½ cup fresh garlic cloves
¼ cup olive oil

Finishing options

tzatziki dip
chopped parsley or mint
white truffle oil

directions marinate the lamb 1 day in advance

To prepare the lamb, make a paste from the first 7 ingredients. Rub it all over the lamb, and wrap the meat tightly in plastic wrap. Marinate overnight in the refrigerator.

Remove the lamb from the refrigerator 2 hours prior to cooking and let it rest. Meanwhile, preheat a grill.

Cook the meat, turning often, until the internal temperature reaches 120°. (You can also roast the lamb at 350° for approximately 12 minutes per pound.) Allow the meat to cool completely, then slice or shave it thinly from the bone.

Preheat the oven to 350°. Place the sliced lamb in a baking dish, toss well, cover it with foil and bake until the meat is golden and tender.

To prepare the hummus, place all the ingredients, including the juice from the beans, in a food processor and blend until smooth. Season with salt and pepper to taste.

To prepare the pita chips, cut pita pockets into 8 wedges. Mist them with olive oil. Spray a cookie sheet with Pam, lay out the pita wedges in a single layer, and bake at 350° until the chips are crisp, approximately 12-15 minutes.

To serve, spread some hummus on a pita chip and top it with sliced lamb. Garnish, if desired, with tzatziki dip, chopped parsley or mint, or a drizzle of white truffle oil, and serve.

pair with windsor oaks zinfandel, malbec or cabernet sauvignon

soups

Camellia Cellars

57 front street, healdsburg, ca 95448
707-433-1290

www.camelliacellars.com

I found the original recipe for this soup in a Williams-Sonoma cookbook, and simplified it a lot. I came up with the variation for Thai Style Pumpkin Soup because I'm eating tons of fresh Thai food these days. Feel free to adjust the seasonings any way you'd like, according to your tastes—including adding and subtracting the amount of stock, pumpkin, cream and coconut milk, depending on how thick you want the soup. **Serves 6**

soups

pumpkin soup

two ways

chef Chris Lewand

ingredients

Base Recipe

¼ cup unsalted butter
1 large yellow onion, finely chopped
4 cups low-salt chicken broth,
or vegetable stock to make it vegetarian
1 large can pumpkin puree
1 bay leaf
2 tablespoons orange zest, grated
2 tablespoons fresh orange juice
1 tablespoon fresh lemon juice
1 teaspoon fresh ginger, grated
1 teaspoon fresh nutmeg, grated
salt and ground white pepper, to taste

Savory Pumpkin Soup

1-½ cups light cream
¾ pound Gruyére cheese, shredded
fresh chives, chopped

Thai Style Pumpkin Soup

1-½ cups coconut milk
1-½ teaspoon Sriracha hot chili sauce
fresh cilantro leaves, chopped
peanuts, chopped

directions

For both variations: In a large pot, sauté the onion in melted butter until the onion turns light gold. Add the stock, pumpkin and bay leaf. Bring the mixture to a boil, then turn down the heat to simmer for 20 minutes.

Discard the bay leaf. Add the orange zest, orange juice, lemon juice, nutmeg, and ginger. For the savory version, add the cream and most of the cheese to the base recipe. Stir the soup over low heat, until the cheese melts and blends in. Taste and season with salt and pepper. Serve hot, garnished with chives and the remaining cheese. For the Thai version, add the coconut milk and Sriracha sauce to the base soup. Taste and correct the seasonings. Serve hot or cold, with cilantro and peanuts for garnish.

pair the *savory soup* with camellia cellars petite sirah or cabernet sauvignon;
serve the *thai style soup* with camellia cellars first kiss or zinfandel

Chalk Hill Estate Vineyards & Winery

10300 chalk hill road, healdsburg, ca 95448
707-838-4306

www.chalkhill.com

Prepare the crispy fried shallots before starting on the velouté; they can be stored in the refrigerator for up to one week in an airtight container. Double or triple the recipe and use the shallots to add crunch to other dishes. In some stores, Jerusalem artichokes are labeled as sunchokes. **Serves 4**

jerusalem artichoke velouté

with chives & crispy fried shallots

chef Didier Ageorges, Executive Chef

ingredients

Crispy Fried Shallots
6 shallots
vegetable oil

Velouté
2 tablespoons butter
2 teaspoons fresh garlic, chopped
$1/3$ cup onion, chopped
1 pound Jerusalem artichokes, washed, peeled and sliced ¼-inch thick
2 cups chicken stock
1 cup cream
salt and pepper, to taste
1 teaspoon chives, chopped

directions

To prepare the crispy fried shallots, peel and slice the shallots as thinly as possible, using a mandoline or a very sharp knife. On a large sheet tray, spread out the sliced shallots in a thin layer, overlapping as little as possible so that they don't clump during frying.

Pour vegetable oil into a small heavy saucepan, to a depth of 1 inch. Heat the oil over medium-high heat. Add the shallots and fry, stirring constantly, until they are light golden brown, about 90 seconds. Remove the shallots with a slotted spoon and drain them on paper towels. Let cool.

To prepare the velouté, melt the butter in a medium-size saucepan over high heat. Add the garlic and onion and cook until they're soft, about 2 minutes. Add the artichokes and sauté them for 2 minutes. Add the stock and simmer until the chokes are tender.

Add the cream and bring the mixture to a boil. Season with salt and pepper. Puree the mixture in a blender until smooth, strain through a fine sieve, and keep warm. When ready to serve, garnish the soup with a sprinkle each of the fried shallots and chopped chives.

pair with chalk hill estate chardonnay or north slope pinot gris

Christie Estate Winery & Vineyard

54 front street, healdsburg, ca 95448
707-433-3097

www.christievineyards.com

Our clam chowdah is slammin'! Packed with clams,
this recipe is from our own winemaker/clam digger,
Steve Aitken. His celebrated soup pairs perfectly
with Christie Estate's white wines. For convenience
and year-round enjoyment of this chowder,
the recipe calls for canned clams, yet feel free
to use fresh manila clams. **Serves 4-6**

steve's famous

clam chowder

chef Steve Aitken

ingredients

2 tablespoons butter
2 strips bacon, diced
2 carrots, chopped
½ medium yellow onion, chopped
2 celery ribs, chopped
1-2 Yukon Gold potatoes, diced
2 6-½-ounce cans chopped clams
3 to 4 cups bottled clam juice
2 tablespoons flour
3 cups whole milk or half and half
salt and pepper, to taste

directions

In a large stock pot, melt the butter, add the bacon, carrots, onion, celery and potatoes, and sauté until the vegetables are tender. Add the clams and clam juice and bring to a simmer.

Add the flour and the milk or half and half, mix thoroughly, season with salt and pepper, and continue to stir until the chowder reaches the desired consistency. Ladle into bowls.

pair with christie vineyards sauvignon blanc or chardonnay

Dawn Ranch Lodge & Roadhouse Restaurant

16467 river road, guerneville, ca 95446
707-869-0656

www.dawnranch.com

(This recipe is truly best when juicy, vine-ripened tomatoes are available. It's just as delicious at room temperature as it is chilled. **Serves 12**)

tomato gazpacho

ingredients

15 medium ripe tomatoes, cut in half
2 cucumbers, peeled, seeded and chopped
1 red onion, chopped
2 small red bell peppers, seeded and chopped
1 jalapeño, seeded and chopped
4 cloves garlic, chopped
2 tablespoons extra virgin olive oil
½ cup lemon juice
½ cup croutons
1 quart vegetable stock
2 cups V8 juice
Tapatio hot sauce
salt and pepper, to taste

directions

Place all the ingredients except for the hot sauce, salt and pepper in a large bowl and toss well.

Working in batches of approximately 2 cups each, blend the mixture in a food processor until the texture is slightly chunky.

Season with a splash of Tapatio sauce, and salt and pepper to taste, then serve. Alternately, chill for 4 hours before serving.

pair with longboard sauvignon blanc or korbel natural champagne

DeLoach Vineyards

1791 olivet road, santa rosa, ca 95401
707-526-9111

www.deloachvineyards.com

Food and wine are a magical combination—each
one enhancing the other in such delectable ways.
To celebrate this, we encourage our guests to
continually explore and experience the subtleties
of food and wine pairings. We love nothing more
than to prepare luscious meals and pair them
with DeLoach Vineyards wines! **Makes 10 cups**

garden provençal
vegetable soup

chef Sue Boy

ingredients

1 medium onion, chopped
1 small leek, chopped
1 medium carrot, peeled and chopped
1 large celery stalk, chopped
2 medium ripe tomatoes, peeled, seeded and chopped
1 small potato, peeled and chopped
8 cups chicken or vegetable stock
2 teaspoons salt
1 pinch saffron (optional)
1 can white beans, rinsed and drained
1 cup orzo (or other small pasta)
1 small zucchini, quartered lengthwise and sliced
4 ounces green beans, cut into 1-inch pieces
Parmesan cheese, grated (to finish)

Pistou
2 cups fresh basil leaves
3 cloves garlic, chopped
¼ cup extra virgin olive oil

directions

For the soup, in a frying pan, sauté the onion, leek, carrot and celery for 5 to 10 minutes, until the vegetables are slightly soft. Stir in the tomatoes and potato. Add the stock, salt and saffron (if using) and bring the mixture to a boil. Reduce the heat and simmer for 30 minutes.

Add the white beans, orzo, zucchini and green beans, and simmer until the pasta is tender, about 10 minutes.

Meanwhile, make the pistou by placing all the ingredients in a blender and pureeing until the texture is smooth.

To serve, remove the soup from the heat and ladle it into warm bowls. Stir in the pistou and a grating of Parmesan cheese.

pair with deloach russian river valley pinot noir or zinfandel

Forchini Vineyards & Winery

5141 dry creek road, healdsburg, ca 95448
707-431-8886

www.forchini.com

Homemade soup, a loaf of crusty bread and favorite cheeses make for an easy yet filling winter meal. Follow with a palate-cleansing, simple tossed green salad and for dessert, serve fresh winter pears. Of course, a bottle of Forchini Zinfandel will make any festive occasion complete! **Serves 6**

zuppa di funghi forchini

(forchini mushroom soup)

chef Vintage Valley Catering

ingredients

1-½ cups Shiitake mushrooms
1-½ cups crimini mushrooms
1-½ cups oyster mushrooms
1/3 cup olive oil
1 cup onions or shallots, chopped
4 cloves garlic, chopped
1 8-ounce stick salted butter
1 cup Forchini Estate Zinfandel
½ cup dried porcini mushrooms
1 tablespoon fresh thyme, chopped
½ cup heavy cream
1 bay leaf
8 cups vegetable stock
1 tablespoon sherry vinegar or sherry wine
croutons, if desired for topping

directions preheat oven to 325°

Chop the fresh mushrooms and set aside.

In an oven-proof dish, add the olive oil, onions (or shallots) and garlic, and roast them in the oven until the onions and garlic are soft.

To a large soup pot, add the butter and melt it over medium-low heat. Add the fresh mushrooms and the roasted onion mixture, and sauté until the mushrooms are tender (don't overcook).

Add the Zinfandel, increase the heat, and simmer a few minutes. Add the rest of the ingredients except for the croutons and gently simmer for 30 minutes.

To serve, remove the bay leaf and ladle the soup into bowls. Sprinkle croutons on top, if using.

pair with forchini estate zinfandel

Graton Ridge Cellars

3561 gravenstein highway north, sebastopol, ca 95472
707-823-3040

www.gratonridge.com

This substantial soup tastes best when Pinot Noir is used as the wine ingredient, although Zinfandel works well, too. If using Pinot Noir, consider adding 2 ounces of rehydrated dried porcini mushrooms to the soup, to strengthen the bridge between the earthiness of the mushrooms and that of Pinot Noir. **Serves 10**

pinot lentil soup

with sausage

ingredients

1 tablespoon vegetable oil
½ pound mild Italian sausage
1 onion, chopped
2 cloves garlic, crushed
1-½ cups dried lentils, rinsed
6 cups beef, chicken or vegetable stock
1 bay leaf
2 carrots, chopped
3 celery stalks, chopped
2 14-½ ounce cans chopped tomatoes, including juice
1 tablespoon tomato paste
½ cup Pinot Noir
¼ cup lemon juice
2 tablespoon Worcestershire sauce
1 tablespoon brown sugar
½ teaspoon black pepper
salt to taste
chopped green onion and/or fresh parsley, for garnish

directions

In a 4-quart pot, heat the oil over medium heat. Add the sausage and brown it for 10 minutes, breaking up the meat with the back of a spoon. Stir in the onion and garlic, and sauté for 10 minutes.

Stir in the lentils, stock, bay leaf, carrots, celery, tomatoes with their juices and tomato paste. Bring the mixture to a boil, reduce the heat, and simmer 1 hour.

Remove the bay leaf and stir in the wine, lemon juice, Worcestershire sauce, sugar and pepper, and simmer the soup for 30 more minutes. Taste the soup and adjust the salt and pepper, if needed.

Ladle the soup into warm bowls and garnish with the chopped green onion and/or chopped fresh parsley, if desired.

pair with graton ridge russian river valley pinot noir

Harvest Moon Estate & Winery

2192 olivet road, santa rosa, ca 95401
707-573-8711

www.harvestmoonwinery.com

This soul-warming soup has a spicy kick, thanks to the inclusion of a small amount of sauce from a can of chipotles en adobo. The chiles can be found in the Hispanic section of most supermarkets. **Serves 4-6**

butternut squash soup

with chipotle

ingredients

1 medium yellow onion, roughly chopped
¼ pound unsalted butter
1 medium butternut squash, peeled, seeded and cut into
1-inch cubes
2 sprigs thyme
1 teaspoon ground cumin
1 quart water (approximate)
2 tablespoons orange juice concentrate
1 tablespoon sauce from 1 can of chipotles en adobo
salt and white pepper, to taste

directions

In a stock pot, combine the chopped onion and butter, and heat over medium heat until the onions are translucent. Add the butternut squash, thyme, cumin and just enough water to cover the squash.

Bring the mixture to a simmer, and cook until the squash falls off a fork when speared. Remove the sprigs of thyme.

With the pot still on the heat, use a submersible blender to blend the soup until it's smooth. Keep the soup at a simmer and add the orange juice concentrate, chipotle sauce and the salt and white pepper. Taste the soup and adjust the seasoning as needed.

pair with your favorite harvest moon wine

Hobo Wine Company

132 plaza street, healdsburg, ca 95448
707-473-0337

www.hobowines.com

Terrapin Creek Café in Bodega Bay created this recipe,
which features kuri squash (also called Japanese squash),
a tear-shaped winter squash with reddish-orange flesh
and a nutty flavor. Vegetarians and carnivores alike will
love this complex, slightly spicy soup. **Serves 8-10**

curry kuri squash soup

ingredients

5 pounds kuri squash
2 yellow onions, sliced
5 garlic cloves, smashed
1 tablespoon prepared yellow curry paste
1 cup dry white wine
1 quart vegetable stock or water
1 cup coconut milk
1 cinnamon stick
pinch nutmeg
salt and pepper, to taste

directions preheat oven to 350°

Cut the kuri squashes in half and scrape out the seeds. Place each half on a baking tray, cut down side, and roast 30 minutes, or until tender.

Meanwhile, in a large pot, add the onion, garlic and curry paste, and sweat until the onions are tender. Add the white wine and cook until about half the liquid evaporates. Add the vegetable stock or water, and bring to a simmer.

When the kuri squash is tender, scrape out the flesh and add it to the pot. Add the coconut milk, cinnamon, nutmeg, salt and pepper, and simmer for about 10 minutes.

Carefully take out the cinnamon stick, and transfer the mixture, in batches if necessary, to a blender or food processor. Blend until the soup is smooth, adjust the seasoning, and serve.

pair with banyan gewürztraminer

Kendall-Jackson, Healdsburg

337 healdsburg avenue, healdsburg, ca 95448
707-433-7102

www.kj.com

The natural sweetness in sunchokes, also known as Jerusalem artichokes, balances the tartness of the Granny Smith apple in this light pureed soup. An optional splash of cream in the soup enhances the buttery finish in the wine. Verjus—unfermented, under-ripe grape juice—is available in gourmet stores and at some wineries; apple cider vinegar may be substituted. **Serves 6-8**

soups

granny smith apple soup

with sunchokes

chef Ryan Pollnow

ingredients

1 ounce butter
½ yellow onion, cut into small dice
1 pound sunchokes, peeled and cut into small pieces
½ pound Granny Smith apples, peeled, cored and cut into small pieces
water, as needed
1 cup Chardonnay verjus (or 1 tablespoon apple cider vinegar)
1 tablespoon honey
¼ cup cream (optional)
kosher salt to taste

directions

In a large saucepan over medium heat, melt the butter, add the onions, and turn down the heat to medium-low. Stir the mixture occasionally and cook until the onions are tender, approximately 8 minutes.

Add the sunchokes, apples and enough water to cover. Add the verjus (or cider vinegar) and honey, and turn the heat to high. When the soup comes to a boil, reduce the heat and simmer it for 35 minutes.

Carefully transfer the soup to a blender and process it until it's smooth. If desired, top with the cream and season with salt. Serve hot.

pair with kendall-jackson camelot highlands chardonnay

Kokomo Winery

4791 dry creek road, healdsburg, ca 95448
707-433-0200

www.kokomowines.com

Started in 2004, Kokomo Winery (named after winemaker
Erik Miller's hometown) focuses on both Dry Creek and
Russian River Valley fruit. We think you should drink local and
think global, and we are proud to support various causes we
believe in throughout Sonoma and Marin counties. **Serves 12-16**

smoked chicken &
corn chowder

chef Scott Grove

ingredients

1 cup onion, sliced
1 tablespoon butter
2 tablespoons olive oil
1-½ cups onion, minced
1 cup celery, diced
¾ cup carrot, diced
½ cup fennel, minced
1 tablespoon garlic, minced
1 cup Kokomo Sauvignon Blanc
1 quart water
1 quart chicken stock
2 cups russet potatoes, diced
3 cups smoked corn, shucked
3 cups smoked chicken, diced

1 pint heavy cream
1-½ tablespoons Thai basil, chopped
1-½ tablespoons lemon thyme, chopped
1-½ tablespoons fresh oregano, chopped
¼ cup Parmigiano-Reggiano cheese, grated
¼ cup Manchego cheese, grated
2 tablespoons Worcestershire sauce
2 tablespoons rice wine vinegar
1 teaspoon ground cumin
1 teaspoon ground coriander
salt and pepper, to taste
bacon bits
Thai basil oil

directions

In a large stockpot over medium heat, sauté the sliced onion with the butter for 25-30 minutes, until the onions are caramelized. Set them aside, measuring out ½ cup.

Wipe the stockpot clean, add the olive oil, and on high heat, sauté the uncooked minced onions, celery, carrots, fennel and garlic until they're soft. Deglaze the pot with the white wine, reduce the heat, and simmer until just 2 tablespoons of liquid remain.

Add the water, stock, potatoes, corn and chicken. Bring to a boil. Reduce the heat and let simmer 30 minutes, stirring frequently. Add the cream and fresh chopped herbs, and bring back to a boil. Reduce the heat and let the mixture simmer 20 minutes.

Bring the soup back to a boil, and thicken it with some cornstarch mixed with water. Add the reserved caramelized onions, grated cheeses, Worcestershire sauce, rice wine vinegar, cumin, coriander, salt and pepper. Heat through, ladle the chowder into bowls and garnish with bacon bits and a drizzle of Thai basil oil.

pair with zinfandel

Lynmar Estate

3909 frei road, sebastopol, ca 95472
707-829-3374

www.lynmarestate.com

Last year we had an incredible harvest of tomatoes on the estate. I hoped to develop a soup recipe to match with our Pinot Noirs, yet the natural acidity in the tomatoes can clash with red wine. I found that alliums (which include onions, garlic, leeks and chives) added a creamy component to the soup, and downplayed the acidity. The addition of brown sugar softened the acid even more. This recipe offers a bonus: The tomato puree can be frozen and used to make the soup throughout the winter. **Serves 16**

soups

heirloom tomato soup

with leeks, sweet onions, garlic & chive crème fraiche

chef Sandra Simile

ingredients

Heirloom Tomato Puree

1 gallon (16 cups) heirloom tomatoes,
washed and coarsely chopped

Soup

2 tablespoons olive oil
2 tablespoons butter
4 cups leeks, cleaned, trimmed and thinly sliced
4 cups sweet onions, small dice
3 tablespoons garlic, finely chopped
2 tablespoons lemon thyme, finely chopped
1 tablespoon marjoram, finely chopped
12 cups heirloom tomato puree (see recipe)
2 tablespoons brown sugar
salt and pepper, to taste
1 cup crème fraiche
2 tablespoons chives, very finely minced

directions

To prepare the heirloom puree, place the tomatoes in a large stainless steel pot, cover and bring to a boil. Reduce to a simmer and cook about 20 minutes, or until the tomatoes are very soft. Take the pot off the heat and put the tomatoes through a food mill to remove the seeds and skins. Measure out 12 cups for this recipe, and freeze the remainder for future use.

To prepare the soup, in a wide, 5-quart pot, add the oil, butter, leeks and onions, and sauté on low heat for 5 minutes. Add the garlic, stir well, cover, and cook for another 15 minutes, until the mixture is very soft. Remove the lid, add the thyme and marjoram, and cook 3 minutes more.

Finely puree the leek/onion mixture in a food processor and return it to the pot. Whisk in the tomato puree. Bring the mixture to a simmer, and cook for 5 minutes.

Add the brown sugar and stir well to combine. Add salt and pepper to taste. Mix the crème fraiche and chives together in a small bowl.

To serve, ladle the soup into warm bowls, topping each with ½ tablespoon of crème fraiche/chive blend.

pair with lynmar russian river valley pinot noir

Pedroncelli Winery

1220 canyon road, geyserville, ca 95441
707-857-3531

www.pedroncelli.com

This is one of our favorite dishes from our go-to, wine-friendly recipe resource: "Zinfandel Cookbook: Food to go with California's Heritage Wine," by Jan Nix and Margaret Smith. We added crusty Costeaux Bakery bread and Vella Mezzo Secco Dry Jack cheese, and renamed it in honor of our flagship Zinfandel wine. **Serves 6**

zinion soup

ingredients

2 tablespoons butter
1 tablespoon olive oil
4 large mild onions, thinly sliced
1 tablespoon all-purpose flour
6 cups reduced-sodium beef broth
½ cup Pedroncelli Mother Clone Zinfandel
salt and pepper to taste
6 slices crusty Costeaux French bread, toasted
1 cup Vella Mezzo Secco Dry Jack cheese, grated

directions preheat oven to 350°

In a wide, deep frying pan, melt the butter with the oil over medium heat. Add the onions and cook, stirring occasionally, until the onions are soft and have a rich caramel color, about 30-40 minutes.

Stir in the flour and cook, stirring constantly, for 1 minute. Add the broth and wine, and simmer for 10 minutes. Season to taste with salt and freshly ground pepper.

To finish the soup, ladle it into oven-proof bowls. Float a piece of the toasted bread in each bowl and sprinkle with the cheese. Heat the soup in the oven until the cheese melts, about 10 minutes.

pair with pedroncelli mother clone zinfandel

Rosenblum Cellars

250 center street, healdsburg, ca 95448
707-431-1169

www.rosenblumcellars.com

Founded in 1978, Rosenblum Cellars, a well-known Zinfandel producer, will work with Chef Mike Matson from a local Healdsburg catering company, Vintage Valley, to masterfully pair his zesty white bean soup with its Rockpile Zin. **Serves 8-10**

soups

italian sausage &
white bean soup

chef Mike Matson, Vintage Valley Catering

ingredients

3 pounds Italian sausage Links
2 cups carrots, diced
2 cups celery, diced
2 cups shallots, diced
½ bottle Rosenblum Zinfandel
2 pounds white Navy beans
1 quart chicken stock
¼ cup lemon juice
1 bunch thyme, chopped
2 bay leaves
1 tablespoon chili paste
salt and pepper, to taste
toasted bread crumbs (optional)

directions

Slice the sausage and brown it in a large pot. Set the sausage aside.

In the same pot, add the carrots, celery and shallots, heat them until they begin to sweat, and add the Zinfandel.

Cook until the mixture is reduced by half, and add the rest of ingredients, including the browned sausage. Simmer the soup until the beans are tender.

Remove the bay leaves, pour the soup into warm bowls, and garnish with toasted bread crumbs, if desired.

pair with rosenblum rockpile road zinfandel

Toad Hollow Vineyards

409-a healdsburg avenue, healdsburg, ca 95448
707-431-8667

www.toadhollow.com

Debbie Rickards from our tasting room made this soup for her son,
Matt, every year for his birthday. His favorite birthday dinner was
potato soup and hamburgers; Debbie added the white truffle oil and
chives later, for a dish more suited to adult tastes. **Serves 8-10**

soups

potato leek soup

with white truffle oil & chives

chef Debbie Rickards

ingredients

6 large leeks
1 stick butter
5-6 shallots, thinly sliced
1 onion, thinly sliced
4-5 garlic cloves, minced
8-10 sprigs fresh thyme
4-5 sprigs fresh Italian parsley
2-3 large russet potatoes, peeled and sliced
4 bay leaves
6-10 black peppercorns, whole
8-10 cups chicken stock (homemade is best)
1-½ cups heavy cream
salt and pepper, to taste
1 large bunch chives, chopped
white truffle oil (use sparingly)

directions

Wash the leeks thoroughly and trim off and discard the dark-green ends; use only the white and light-green parts, and slice them thin.

In a large saucepan, melt the butter. Sauté the sliced leeks, shallots and onion over medium heat, until they are soft and tender. Do not allow to brown — you want this soup to be white. Add the garlic and continue to sauté for about 1 or 2 more minutes.

Tie the sprigs of thyme and parsley together in a bunch. Add the herb bunch, potatoes, bay leaves and whole peppercorns to the pot. Cook for 4-6 minutes longer. Add the chicken stock and simmer for 30-40 minutes, until the potatoes are soft. Turn off the heat and let the soup rest for 20 minutes.

Remove the herbs, bay leaves and peppercorns. Puree the mixture until smooth, using a submersion blender, and return the pot to low heat. Add the heavy cream. Simmer until the soup thickens a bit. Add salt and pepper to taste, and garnish each serving with a sprinkle of chopped chives and a *light* drizzle of white truffle oil.

pair with toad hollow francine's selection unoaked chardonnay

salads & sides

Hanna Winery

9280 highway 128, healdsburg, ca 95448
707-431-4310

5353 occidental road, santa rosa, ca 95401
707-575-3371

www.hannawinery.com

This is my favorite fall salad. The earthiness of the lentils and prosciutto play off the color and sweetness of autumn's bounty of peppers. I love this salad served with duck, but it works equally well with chicken and fish. Best of all, it can be served at room temperature, and tastes even better the next day. Make it the day before, throw some meat on the grill, pop a few corks, and enjoy the late fall sunshine!. **Serves 6-8**

french lentil & prosciutto salad

with peppers

chef Chris Hanna

ingredients

6 paper-thin slices of Prosciutto di Parma, chopped
2 shallots, minced
½ cup carrots, diced
½ cup red pepper, diced
2 cups French green lentils, rinsed and drained
¼ cup fresh parsley, chopped
2 teaspoons fresh thyme, chopped
2 tablespoons red wine vinegar
1 tablespoon Dijon mustard
⅓ cup olive oil
salt and pepper, to taste

directions

Sauté the prosciutto in a heavy saucepan over medium heat, until lightly browned. Add the shallots and sauté until translucent. Add the carrot and pepper, and sauté for a few minutes more, until the vegetables are al dente. Reserve.

In a medium saucepan, bring the lentils to a boil in at least a quart of water, then reduce the heat to medium-low. Cover and simmer until the lentils are tender, about 30 minutes. Drain, then transfer the lentils to a large bowl. Add the reserved prosciutto and vegetable mixture, along with the parsley and thyme, and combine.

Whisk the vinegar and mustard in small bowl. Drizzle in olive oil until it emulsifies, add salt and pepper to taste, and toss the salad with dressing. Correct the seasoning as needed.

pair with hanna pinot noir

Johnson's Alexander Valley Wines

8333 highway 128, healdsburg, ca 95448
707-433-2319

www.johnsonavwines.com

This salad tastes best when made a day or two in advance, after the flavors have melded. It feeds a crowd, so serve it at your next party. Marie's Greek Vinaigrette can be found in the refrigerated produce section of most supermarkets. **Serves 10**

couscous & feta salad

with olives

chef Ellen Johnson

ingredients

3 boxes garlic and olive oil couscous
2 cups cherry tomatoes, sliced in half
1 5-ounce jar kalamata olives, drained
1 cup mixed-color bell peppers, diced
1 large cucumber, peeled and diced
1 cup fresh parsley, finely chopped
10 ounces crumbled feta cheese
1 to 1-½ cups Marie's Greek Vinaigrette

directions

Prepare the couscous as directed on the package. Let it cool to room temperature, stirring occasionally with a fork to separate clumps.

Add the remaining ingredients, mix well and chill overnight.

pair with johnson's alexander valley chardonnay

Matrix Winery

3291 westside road, healdsburg, ca 95448
707-433-1911

www.matrixwinery.com

Costeaux French Bakery in Healdsburg, owned by the
Seppi family since 1981, is known for its extraordinary
breads and pastries, as well as the family's support
of community causes. Will Seppi is most generous in
sharing Costeaux's focaccia recipe with us (and you).
Use it as the foundation for hearty sandwiches, or
simply dip it in local extra virgin olive oil. **Serves 8-10**

costeaux focaccia

ingredients

2 cups bread flour
¼ teaspoon salt
2 teaspoons olive oil
¾ cup whole milk
1-¼-ounce package fresh active yeast, crumbled
olive oil for brushing the focaccia
salt for seasoning

directions preheat oven to 400°

Combine the first 5 ingredients in a large bowl. Mix by hand or with an electric mixer fitted with a dough hook, for 8-12 minutes, until the mixture is well-combined. Finish by hand, kneading the dough until it's smooth. Remove the dough to a clean bowl and cover it with plastic wrap or a clean cloth, then place it in a warm spot (preferably 75° or higher). Let the dough double in size.

Remove the dough from the bowl and divide it in half. Place each piece on a sheet pan or pizza stone and fatten and dimple the dough with your hands and fingers to make approximately 2 10-inch rounds. Brush each round with olive oil and top with a sprinkling of salt. Bake until done, approximately 30 to 40 minutes.

pair with matrix pinot noir

pasta & rice

Merriam Vineyards

11654 los amigos road, healdsburg, ca 95448
707-433-4032

www.merriamvineyards.com

Bombolotti is a ridged tube pasta, similar to rigatoni, and it's terrific for trapping all the mushrooms and savory juices of this hearty dish. If you can't find bombolotti, small rigatoni is a fine substitute. **Serves 4**

portobello mushroom bombolotti

with bacon & hazelnuts

chef Mark Stark, Chef / Owner, Willi's Seafood & Raw Bar

ingredients

1 slice thick-cut bacon, diced
1 yellow onion, peeled and diced
1 carrot, peeled and diced
1 stalk celery, peeled and diced
kosher salt and fresh-ground black pepper
1 clove garlic, peeled and minced
8 ounces portobello mushrooms, stemmed, gills cleaned, diced
1 tablespoon fresh thyme leaves, minced
1 tomato, seeded and diced (fresh or quality canned)
1 cup mushroom stock, or canned reduced-sodium chicken broth
12 ounces dried bombolotti pasta (or small rigatoni)
2 tablespoons freshly grated Parmigiano-Reggiano cheese
¼ cup crushed toasted hazelnuts

directions

For the mushroom sauce, render the bacon in a large skillet until crispy. Add the onion, carrot, celery, salt and pepper, and cook, stirring occasionally, until the vegetables begin to soften, about 5 minutes. Add additional oil if needed.

Add the garlic and cook for 1 minute, then add the mushrooms and thyme leaves. Cook, stirring frequently, until the mushrooms are almost tender, about 3 minutes. Add the tomato, cook about 2 minutes more, then add the stock, 2 tablespoons at a time, bringing the pan to a simmer before each addition.

Simmer the sauce until it is concentrated but not yet dry, about 30 minutes. Set aside until the pasta is cooked.

For the pasta, bring a large pot of water to a boil and season well with salt. Add the pasta and cook according to the directions on the package. When the pasta is cooked, drain it and place it back in the cooking pot. Add the mushroom sauce and reheat, then stir in the crushed hazelnuts and season with salt and pepper to taste.

To serve, place the pasta in 4 bowls and sprinkle with the grated Parmigiano-Reggiano.

pair with merriam miktos bordeaux-style blend

Raymond Burr Vineyards

8339 west dry creek road, healdsburg, ca 95448
707-433-8559

www.raymondburrvineyards.com

(When I was a little girl, my father would make this sauce for Saturday night dinner, so my mom could have a night off from household duties. He would make it early in the morning, and we would smell the sauce cooking all day long. We were never late for dinner! **Serves 6-8**)

pasta & rice

sugo di carne

(meat sauce)

chef Sue Nelson

ingredients

¼ cup butter
½ cup olive oil
½ pound ground beef
3 slices bacon, chopped
1 celery stalk, chopped
1 medium onion, chopped
1 cup Raymond Burr Cabernet Sauvignon
salt and pepper, to taste
1 tablespoon flour
1 cup white mushrooms, sliced
1 16-ounce can Italian-style tomatoes, chopped
1 16-ounce can tomato sauce
1 bay leaf
1 teaspoon thyme
your favorite pasta
freshly grated Parmigiano-Reggiano cheese

directions

In a large saucepan, combine half of the butter and all of the olive oil. Heat, then add the ground beef and bacon, and brown. Add the celery and onion, and cook for 10 minutes.

Add the wine, salt and pepper, and cook for 10 minutes.

Mix the remaining butter with the flour and add it to the sauce, stirring well. Then add the mushrooms, tomatoes, tomato sauce, bay leaf and thyme. Cover and simmer on gentle heat for 1 hour.

Remove the bay leaf, and serve the sauce over pasta. Top with grated Parmigiano-Reggiano.

pair with raymond burr cabernet sauvignon

Selby Winery

215 center street, healdsburg, ca 95448
707-431-1288

www.selbywinery.com

"This recipe is the result of many years of toiling for the perfect Bolognaise," says chef Sean Thompson. "Each time I made a change, I would take it to my mentor, an elderly woman from Bologna, who would taste it and give me her advice. 'It's too saucy,' she would say, or, 'it's too bland.' Finally one day, she said it was 'perfetto,' and this is the recipe that won her approval." **Serves 8**

selby bolognese

chef Sean Thompson

ingredients

2 pounds ground beef
1 pound hot Italian sausage
2 cups yellow onion, diced
½ cup garlic, chopped
¼ cup dried oregano
⅛ cup dried basil
2 tablespoons sea salt
2 tablespoons ground black pepper
2 tablespoons whole fennel seed
½ teaspoon red chile flakes
4 bay leaves
2 cups Selby Dolcetto
2 28-ounce cans tomato sauce
1 28-ounce can tomato puree

directions

In a large saucepot, brown the ground beef and sausage, breaking them up into large pieces. Drain off the grease and return to the pan. Add the onion and garlic, and cook for 3 minutes. Then add the other spices, bay leaves and the Selby Dolcetto, and mix well. Add the tomato sauce and tomato puree, and simmer for 1 hour.

Remove the bay leaves, and serve over pasta or polenta.

pair with selby russian river valley dolcetto

Sheldon Wines

6761 sebastopol avenue, #500, sebastopol, ca 95472
707-829-8100

www.sheldonwines.com

I picked up this recipe when Tobe and I stayed in a little village in the Italian Alps. There was a lovely "refuge" (restaurant/inn) that could be accessed only by hiking 4 hours into the Dolomites, at 9,000 feet elevation. The refuge served this amazing truffled risotto with a tasty young Pinot Nero right from the barrel. We sat in this 200-year-old lodge, by the big roaring fire, with views all the way to Austria. This recipe honors that experience – without the long walk back. **Serves 4**

pasta & rice

truffle cheese risotto

chef Dylan Sheldon

ingredients

1 medium yellow onion
1 stick butter
3 cups chicken stock
1 cup arborio rice
½ cup dry white wine
½ cup Parmigiano Reggiano, grated
⅓ cup Cacio di Bosco al Tartufo (Italian truffle Pecorino), grated
salt and pepper, to taste
small sprig of fresh thyme

directions

Coarsely chop the onion. Heat a large, thick-bottomed stock pot, add all but 1 tablespoon of the butter and the onions, and simmer until the onions are translucent, stirring occasionally.

In a separate pot, warm the chicken stock. Add the rice to the pot with the onions, and toast the rice for a minute or two, stirring constantly. The rice will roughly quadruple in size by the time the risotto is done.

Next, add the white wine to the rice. Stir constantly. Once about half the wine is absorbed by the rice, use a ladle to slowly add the chicken broth to the rice, stirring constantly. As the broth is absorbed by the rice, add more. Taste the rice occasionally to get a sense of how done it is. When it's nearly done, the starches will have been released, creating a rich, creamy concoction. The rice will be mostly soft, with a tiny bit of hardness in the center.

Cut the remaining 1 tablespoon of butter into thirds and, one by one, drop the chunks into the risotto, stirring to meld. Add the Parmigiano Reggiano, stir into the risotto for a minute or two, then stir in the truffle cheese. Turn off the heat, stir until well incorporated, and garnish with the thyme and a shaving of Parmigiano Reggiano.

pair with sheldon pinot noir

entrées

Acorn Winery/Alegría Vineyards

12040 old redwood highway, healdsburg, ca 95448
707-433-6440

www.acornwinery.com

(Acorn Winery is named to honor the many old oak trees
in our vineyards, for the oak used in the barrels where our
wines mature, and in recognition of our very small size. The
vineyard's name, Alegría, means joy. Working in the vineyards
makes us happy, and we hope that drinking wines made
from our grapes will bring alegría to your life. **Serves 4**)

entrées

duck & mushroom ragu

on acorn squash polenta

chef Jeff Mall, Chef / Owner, Zin Restaurant & Wine Bar

ingredients

Duck Ragu

4 whole duck legs
kosher salt and black pepper, to taste
2 tablespoons olive oil
½ pound mixed wild mushrooms
4 shallots, minced
2 cloves garlic, chopped
1 bunch fresh thyme, chopped
1-½ cups Acorn Heritage Vines Zinfandel
1-½ cups duck or chicken stock
1 cup San Marzano canned tomatoes, chopped
1 cup pitted green olives, sliced in half
fresh parsley, chopped

Acorn Squash Polenta

3 cups water
2 ounces unsalted butter
salt to taste
¾ cup polenta
2 cups acorn squash, diced and blanched

directions

To prepare the ragu, season the duck legs with salt and pepper. Heat the oil in a large sauté pan over medium heat. Sear the duck legs, skin side down, until they're browned. Turn over and sear the other side. Remove the legs from the pan.

In the same pan, sauté the mushrooms in the duck juices, along with the shallots, garlic and thyme. When the mushrooms have released most of their juices, add the Zinfandel and stock, and bring to a boil.

Return the duck legs to the pan and add the tomatoes and olives. Cover the pan and reduce the heat to a slow simmer. Cook for 1 hour. When the ragu is done, skim off the fat, and season the sauce to taste with salt and pepper.

To prepare the polenta, in a large pot, bring the water to a boil. Add the butter and pinch of salt. Add the polenta, while stirring. Reduce the heat to low and cook for 30 minutes, stirring often. Add the squash and season to taste with salt and pepper.

Serve the duck ragu over the acorn squash polenta, garnished with the chopped parsley.

pair with acorn heritage vines zinfandel or axiom syrah

Alderbrook Winery

2306 magnolia drive, healdsburg, ca 95448
707-433-5987

www.alderbrook.com

This zesty chili is so simple to make, and takes on added flavor if it's served with any number of optional toppings, including grated cheddar cheese, chopped green onions, sour cream and plain non-fat yogurt. **Serves 8-10**

entrées

alderbrook estate chili

chef Michael Monahan

ingredients

2 pounds ground beef
2 cups yellow onion, chopped
2 cloves garlic, minced
1 can diced tomatoes, with juices
1 large can tomato sauce
½ cup Alderbrook Estate Zinfandel
1 cup beef broth
1 can diced green chilies
1-½ tablespoons New Mexican chili powder (or regular chili powder)
½ teaspoon paprika
½ teaspoon sage
½ teaspoon ground cumin
2 teaspoons salt
½ teaspoons fresh ground pepper
4 cans (15 ounces each) red kidney beans, drained

directions

In a large pot over medium heat, brown the meat, onions and garlic, breaking up the meat with a spoon until the beef is no longer pink, and the onions are tender, 6-7 minutes.

Reduce the heat to medium-low, then add the remaining ingredients. Simmer the chili, uncovered, for 30-40 minutes. Serve the chili in warmed bowls, with toppings, if desired.

pair with alderbrook estate zinfandel

Alexander Valley Vineyards

8644 highway 128, healdsburg, ca 95448
707-433-7209

www.avvwine.com

In Argentina, matambre means hunger killer. This dish is served in steak houses throughout the country, as both an appetizer and a main course. As an entree, it is served with warm tortillas. Marinate the meat one day before starting the recipe. **Serves 4-6**

matambre
skirt steak

chef Jeff Young, Culinary Director

ingredients

1 bell pepper, stemmed, seeded and finely chopped
5 cloves garlic, minced
¼ cup olive oil
¼ cup Big Barrel Syrah
1 teaspoon oregano
½ teaspoon red pepper flakes
½ teaspoon salt and pepper
1-½ pounds skirt steak

directions

To prepare the marinade, combine the bell pepper, garlic, oil, wine, oregano, red pepper flakes, salt and pepper. Set aside.

Cut the skirt steak into 3 sections and place them in a non-reactive baking dish. Pour the marinade over the steaks and toss well to coat. Cover the dish and marinate the meat overnight in the refrigerator.

When ready to cook, preheat a grill to high. Remove the steaks from the marinade and season with spice rub. Cook the steaks for 4 minutes on each side. Transfer them to a cutting board and let rest for 5 minutes.

Slice the meat thinly across the grain and serve with warm tortillas and your favorite salsa.

pair with alexander valley school big barrel syrah

Artiste Winery & Tasting Studio

439 healdsburg avenue, healdsburg, ca 95448
707-433-1920

www.artiste.com

Combining a reverence for tradition and a philosophy
of winemaking as an artistic expression, Artiste wines
are labeled with gorgeous works of impressionist
art. Each of our wine blends is named after the title
of the painting that graces its bottle. **Serves 6**

entrées

grilled beef steak

with gorgonzola risotto

chef Todd Muir

ingredients

1 pound beef steak
¼ cup extra virgin olive oil, plus extra for coating
olive oil to brush steaks
salt and pepper, to taste
7-8 cups meat stock, preferably homemade
½ cup onion, minced
3 cup arborio or carnaroli rice
1 cup red or white wine
1 tablespoon fresh parsley, minced
2 tablespoons butter
½ cup crumbled gorgonzola dolce cheese

directions

Brush the steaks with olive oil, then season them generously with salt and pepper. Grill or broil the steaks to medium-rare, about 4-5 minutes per each side, or to desired doneness. Set the steaks aside and keep them warm.

In a large sauce pot, heat the meat stock to a simmer. In a separate pot, heat the ¼ cup extra virgin olive oil. Add the onions and cook until they're soft but not browned, about 3 minutes. Add the rice and heat to coat each grain well with oil. Cook the rice until the grains are translucent, with a white dot in the center, about 3 minutes. Add the wine to the rice and cook until the liquid is completely absorbed.

Set aside ½ cup of the stock to use later in the recipe. Add the rest of the simmering stock, 1 ladle at a time, to the rice. Wait until the stock is completely absorbed before adding the next ladle of stock. When the rice is tender to the bite but still firm in the center, after about 20 minutes, add the parsley, reserved stock, butter and cheese. Season to taste with salt and pepper.

To serve, slice the steaks and arrange on top of the risotto.

pair with artiste ascension red blend

Balletto Vineyards

5700 occidental road, santa rosa, ca 95401
707-568-2455

www.ballettovineyards.com

Located in the southwest area of the Russian River Valley, a portion of the Balletto property edges the border of the Laguna de Santa Rosa, a vital wetland habitat and home to many species of birds and animals. The Ballettos feel this area of land is so beautiful that it should be shared. Working with the Sonoma County Agricultural Preservation & Open Space District, they will preserve this land for all those living in the area, and for visitors to our wonderful county! Future visions include a seasonal trail for all to enjoy. **Serves 8-10**

entrées

zin chili

ingredients

Step 1

8 cups red beans
3-4 pounds hamburger
4 cups tomato sauce
2 cups catsup
2 cups onion, chopped
1 cup celery, chopped
3 cloves garlic

Step 2

1 cup catsup
1 cup tomato puree
½ cup wine vinegar
1 cup Balletto Zinfandel
½ cup chili powder
¼ cup paprika
1 tablespoon oregano
1 tablespoon cumin
1 tablespoon black pepper
1 tablespoon seasoning salt

Cheddar cheese, shredded, to garnish

directions soak 8 cups of red beans overnight

Rinse and drain the soaked beans, place them in a large pot, and add enough water to cover the beans. Mix in the hamburger, tomato sauce, catsup, onions, celery and garlic. Over medium heat, cook the beans until they're tender, 2-3 hours.

Mix together the ingredients in Step 2 and add them to the meat and beans. Simmer an additional 30 minutes.

Spoon the chili into bowls and top with the shredded cheese.

pair with balletto zinfandel

Bella Vineyards & Wine Caves

9711 west dry creek road, healdsburg, ca 95448
707-473-9171

www.bellawinery.com

Sweet Italian sausage paired with a full-bodied Syrah or Zinfandel—what a perfect way to warm up a fall evening. This weekend at Bella, we'll serve this treat in our wine caves, tucked into a steep hillside under our prized Lily Hill vineyard. **Serves 8-10**

entrées

fall sausage wellington

chef Todd Muir

ingredients

½ pound uncooked, sweet Italian sausage, casings removed, chilled
¼ pound ground duck (may substitute ground lamb), chilled
¼ onion, finely chopped
2 tablespoon dried cranberries, chopped
3 large garlic clove, minced
1 teaspoon dried thyme
1 teaspoon kosher salt
1 sheet frozen puff pastry, thawed
1 egg, lightly beaten

directions preheat oven to 400°

Lightly grease a large baking sheet. In a large bowl, combine the sausage, ground duck, onion, cranberries, garlic, thyme and salt. Mix thoroughly.

Place the sausage mix onto aluminum foil and roll the mixture to make sausage-size, long rolls. Place the rolls on an ungreased cookie sheet and bake them for 20-30 minutes, or until cooked. Let cool.

Unroll the sausages from the foil. Unfold the puff pastry sheet on a floured work surface, and roll it out to a 12- by 10-inch rectangle. Cut the pastry crosswise into 3 10- by 4-inch strips. Brush each strip with the beaten egg.

Cut the sausage rolls to fit the pastry. Place the sausage down the center of each pastry strip. Fold the long sides in, covering the sausage and overlapping slightly in the center; press the seams to seal.

Arrange the rolls seam-side down on the prepared sheet. Cover the sheet and put it in the refrigerator until the rolls are firm, at least 10 minutes and up to 1 hour. Raise the oven temperature to 425°. Brush the rolls with the remaining beaten egg, and bake until they are puffed and golden, about 20 minutes.

Cool slightly. Cut each roll crosswise into 8 pieces and serve.

pair with bella zinfandel or syrah

Carol Shelton Wines

3354-b coffey lane, santa rosa, ca 95403
707-575-3441

www.carolshelton.com

Carol has had a long love affair with the food of Chef
Greg Hallihan. Chef Hallihan will prepare this culinary
delight to perfectly pair with our Karma Zinfandel. This
is an opportunity for you to visit a small "urban garage"
winery with lots of character. **Serves 6**

entrées

zinfandel-braised duck

with mascarpone polenta

chef Gregory Hallihan

ingredients

Duck

4 tablespoons vegetable oil
6 whole duck legs
2 medium yellow onions, sliced
2 large shallots, diced
2 medium carrots, diced
2 ribs celery, diced
1 bottle Carol Shelton Karma Zin
2 quarts beef or chicken stock
1 teaspoon salt

Mascarpone Polenta

5 cups water
3 cups milk
3-½ cups polenta
5 tablespoons mascarpone cheese

directions preheat oven to 400°

To prepare the duck, use a large sauté pan with a snug-fitting lid. Heat the pan on medium heat and add the vegetable oil. Salt and pepper the duck legs, then sear the duck in vegetable oil until the legs are medium-brown, turning to brown both sides.

Remove the legs from the pan and in it, lightly sauté the onions, shallots, carrots and celery. Deglaze the pan with the whole bottle of Karma Zin. Return the duck legs to the pan and add the stock and salt. Put the lid on the pan and roast the duck in the oven for 2 hours.

Remove the legs from the braising pot and reduce the liquid by approximately ⅓ by boiling it gently over medium heat. In the meantime, remove the duck meat from the bones, discarding the skin, and return the meat to the liquid.

To prepare the polenta, bring the water and milk to a light boil and stir in the polenta. Keep stirring the polenta throughout the cooking time, at least 45 minutes, with the polenta barely at a boil the entire time. A whisk or a wooden spoon is best for stirring, keeping the polenta from sticking to the bottom of the pan and burning. When the polenta is tender (not chewy), stir in the mascarpone and salt to taste.

To serve, ladle the soft polenta into a large serving bowl, and top with the braised duck meat and the reduced sauce.

pair with carol shelton karma zin russian river valley

Clos du Bois

19410 geyserville avenue, geyserville, ca 95441
707-857-3100

www.closdubois.com

At harvest time in Sonoma County, the Alexander Valley
bustles with activity. When the winemaking team takes
a much needed break, here is one of our favorite
recipes to celebrate the new vintage **Serves 4-6**

entrées

duck bolognese

ingredients

3 duck legs
¾ cup chicken stock
2 sprigs fresh thyme
2 sprigs fresh oregano
kosher salt and freshly ground pepper, to taste
⅓ cup olive oil
1 small onion, minced
1 small carrot, minced
2 stalks celery, minced
4 cloves garlic, minced
½ pound mushrooms, chopped
¾ cup milk
¾ cup Clos du Bois Carignane
1 cup chopped tomatoes (canned can be used if necessary)
2 tablespoons tomato paste

directions preheat oven to 375°

In a baking dish, arrange the duck in a single layer. Pour the stock over the duck and add the thyme and oregano. Cover the dish with foil and bake for about 1-½ hours, until the meat becomes tender and falls off the bone. When it's cool enough to handle, pull the meat into shreds, then chop it into small pieces.

Heat the olive oil in a large, non-reactive saucepan over medium-high heat. Add the onion, carrot, celery and garlic, and cook for 3 minutes. Add the mushrooms and cook for 3 minutes until they begin to brown. Add the shredded duck and milk. Bring to a boil and cook the mixture until the milk is almost fully absorbed.

Add the wine, bring the mixture to a boil, and cook until the liquid is almost fully evaporated. Add the tomatoes and tomato paste. Reduce the heat and cook on a low simmer for 30 minutes. Season the dish to taste with salt and pepper, and serve with your favorite pasta. Top with some freshly grated Parmigiano-Reggiano.

pair with clos du bois old vine carignane

Copain Wines

7800 eastside road, healdsburg, ca 95448
707-836-8822

www.copainwines.com

In classic wine county style, this recipe was given to one of our owners by an Italian neighbor. It was passed to the neighbor by his grandmother, and today, the recipe is more than a century old. We love it because it's an old-world, artisan dish to pair with our old-world-style wines. **Serves 4**

beef stew & polenta

ingredients

Beef Stew

3 pounds beef chuck roast, cubed
(preferably grass-fed, from Black Sheep Farms)
1 green pepper, finely diced
2 onions, finely chopped
1-½ teaspoons dried Italian seasoning
8 ounces tomato sauce
14 ounces stewed tomatoes
½ cup Copain Syrah
salt and pepper, to taste
Parmesan cheese, for grating (optional)

Polenta

½ cup chicken stock
½ cup of water
1 cup Golden Pheasant polenta
½ pound Franklin Teleme cheese
Salt to taste

directions

For the stew, in a frying pan, brown the meat thoroughly. Add the green peppers, onions and Italian seasoning and simmer for 10 minutes. Add the tomato sauce, stewed tomatoes and the Syrah and combine.

Place the mixture in a pressure cooker and cook at 15psi for 20 minutes. Use the natural release method. When the stew is cooked, carefully open the lid of the pressure cooker, allow the steam to release, and season the stew with salt and pepper.

For the polenta, bring the chicken stock and water to a boil in a large pot. Slowly add the polenta to the simmering liquid. Stir frequently until the desired consistency is reached. Add the Teleme.

Spoon the polenta into large, warm bowls, and top with the stew. Add a grating Parmesan cheese, if desired.

pair with copain syrah

Davis Family Vineyards

52 front street, healdsburg, ca 95448
707-433-3858

www.daviswines.com

Guy and Judy Davis' younger son, Cooper, gets credit
for helping chefs Duskie Estes and John Stewart
develop this recipe. For extra flavor, marinate the pork
shoulder in the rub mixture overnight. **Serves 8**

entrées

slow-roasted pork sliders

with salsa verde

chefs Duskie Estes & John Stewart, Zazu & Bovolo

ingredients

Rub

1 lemon, zest and juice
1 bunch fresh rosemary, picked
1 bunch fresh mint, picked
3 garlic cloves, peeled
2 anchovy fillets
pinch of red chili flakes
1 tablespoon olive oil

Pork

1 pork shoulder, bone in, 5-7 pounds
buns of choice

Salsa Verde

2 cups pure olive oil
5 bunches flat leaf parsley, picked
½ cup capers
3 anchovies
2 cloves garlic
2 lemons, zested and juiced
1 orange, zested and juiced
chili flakes to taste

directions preheat oven to 350°

To prepare the rub, combine all the ingredients in a food processor or blender and blend well. Rub the mixture on the pork shoulder, covering all surfaces, and roast it in the oven until the meat pulls apart with tongs, about 3-4 hours.

For the salsa verde, combine all the ingredients in a food processor or blender and blend well.

To assemble a slider, place a tong-full of pork on a bun, add a spoonful of salsa verde, add the top bun, and dig in.

pair with davis family pinot noir

deLorimier Winery

2001 highway 128, geyserville, ca 95441
800-546-7718

www.delorimierwinery.com

This recipe was adapted from one created by our friend,
Greg Ostermann. We like to top the chili with sour cream,
grated cheese and fresh-chopped cilantro. **Serves 4**

grilled rib-eye steak chili

ingredients

1 pound rib-eye steak
1 garlic clove, smashed, for rubbing
kosher salt and pepper, for rubbing
3 tablespoons olive oil
1 large onion, chopped
6 cloves garlic, finely chopped
¼ pound coarse-ground beef
1 cup deLorimier Francis Zinfandel
1 15-ounce can beef stock
3 fire-roasted red peppers, chopped
1 14.5-ounce can red beans
1 tablespoon Mesa Rosa Chipotle Smoky Blend Chili Powder
1 teaspoon Gephardt's Chili Powder
1 teaspoon ground coriander
1 teaspoon cumin
¼ teaspoon oregano
2 teaspoons cilantro, chopped

directions preheat a grill

Rub the steak with the garlic, kosher salt and pepper. Grill the steak until medium doneness, wrap it in foil, and set aside.

In a large frying pan over medium heat, cook the onion and garlic in the olive oil. Add the ground beef and cook until it's browned, about 10 minutes. Drain the excess fat from the pan, then use the wine to de-glaze the pan.

Chop the steak into bite-sized chunks. Add the steak and the remaining ingredients to the pan, mix well, a simmer for 20 minutes, until the flavors are blended.

To serve, spoon the chili into deep bowls and top with sour cream, grated cheese and/or fresh cilantro.

pair with deLorimier Francis Zinfandel

Dutcher Crossing Winery

8533 dry creek road, healdsburg, ca 95448
866-431-2711

www.dutchercrossingwinery.com

(Proprietor Debra Mathy can almost always be found welcoming guests with Dutchess, her Golden Lab winery dog, sidekick and official greeter. For this special event, Debra will share one of her favorite harvest recipes. **Serves 6**)

entrées

artichoke risotto

with lamb tagine

chef Debra Mathy

ingredients

Lamb Tagine

6 pounds leg of lamb
Dry Rub
4 tablespoons paprika
1 tablespoon turmeric
2 tablespoons cumin
1 tablespoon cayenne
4 tablespoons cinnamon
1 tablespoon ground cloves
2 tablespoons cardamom
4 tablespoons salt
2 tablespoons ground ginger
3 tablespoons garlic powder
3 tablespoons ground coriander
4 tablespoons brown sugar

Risotto

2 tablespoons olive oil
1 tablespoon butter
½ cup shallots, chopped
2 tablespoons garlic, chopped
2 cups uncooked arborio rice
½ cup red wine
6 cups chicken broth, heated and divided
¾ cup Asiago cheese, grated
6 ounces marinated artichoke hearts,
chopped with juice
salt and pepper, to taste

directions

To prepare the lamb, mix all the dry rub ingredients together. Rub the spice blend all over the lamb, and allow the meat to rest in the refrigerator for 3 to 4 hours.

Preheat the oven to 225°. Slow-roast the lamb for 8 to 10 hours, until the meat is tender and falls apart. Shred the lamb, and reheat it when the risotto is ready.

To prepare the risotto, heat the oil and butter in a large saucepan over medium heat. Stir in the shallots and garlic and sauté for 2 to 3 minutes. Add the rice and stir well to coat, about 1 minute. Add the wine and allow it to get absorbed by the rice, about 2 to 3 minutes.

Stir in the chicken broth, ½ cup at a time, waiting until the rice absorbs each ½ cup before adding the next ½ cup. Save ¼ cup of broth for later. Cook the rice until it's done yet still firm, about 15 to 20 minutes. Turn off the heat and stir in the remaining ¼ cup of broth, cheese and artichoke hearts.

Top the risotto with the warmed lamb and serve.

pair with dutcher crossing proprietor's reserve cabernet sauvignon

Family Wineries, Dry Creek Valley

4791 dry creek road, healdsburg, ca 95448
707-433-0100

www.familywines.com

One location featuring 6 different wineries! Collier Falls Vineyards, Dashe Cellars, Forth Vineyards, Lago di Merlo Vineyards, Mietz Cellars and Philip Staley Vineyards: more variety, more diversity and more fun! **Serves 8**

entrées

duck & andouille sausage
jambalaya
chef Jeff Mall, Chef / Owner, Zin Restaurant & Wine Bar

ingredients

6 whole duck legs, skin and bones removed
1 ounce olive oil
1 andouille sausage, sliced into small pieces
2 cups yellow onion, small dice
1 cup green bell pepper, small dice
1 cup celery, small dice
1 tablespoon garlic, chopped
2 cups ground tomatoes
½ cup Zinfandel
1 tablespoon kosher salt
3 cups duck or chicken stock
2 bay leaves
1 tablespoon barbecue spice blend
2 cups long grain white rice
salt and pepper, to taste
hot sauce (optional)

directions

Dice the duck legs into 1-inch size pieces. Add the oil to a heavy-bottom stock pot over medium heat, and render the sausage. Add the duck and cook until the meat is browned, stirring often.

Add the onions, peppers, celery and garlic, and cook until they're soft, about 10 minutes. Add the tomatoes, wine, stock, bay leaves, salt and barbecue spice, and bring the mixture to a boil.

Stir in the rice. Cover the pot with a tight-fitting lid and cook the jambalaya for 20 minutes, without removing the lid.

Remove the pot from the heat and let the dish rest for 10 minutes before removing the lid. Season to taste with additional salt, pepper and hot sauce, if using.

pair with a hearty red wine from collier falls vineyards, dashe cellars, forth vineyards, lago di merlo vineyards, mietz cellars or philip staley vineyards

Hawkes Winery

6734 highway 128, healdsburg, ca 95448
707-433-4295

www.hawkeswine.com

This is a dish I've eaten with Mexicans in California, and Texans in Texas, and assorted folks in the Hunter Valley of Australia. I used to drink beer with it, but that was before I went all uptown and discovered water sports and Cabernet Sauvignon. When I pass those guys on the street these days, I act like I don't even know them. Well, that's business, I guess. **Serves 6**

skirt steak tacos

with cabernet smoked chile sauce

chef Jake Hawkes

ingredients

1 large clove garlic, crushed
¼ cup Hawkes Cabernet Sauvignon
1 tablespoon red wine vinegar
1 tablespoon lime juice
¼ cup olive oil
1 teaspoon smoked paprika, or 2 teaspoons canned
chipotle pepper with juices, minced
1 teaspoon salt
½ teaspoon crushed black pepper
1 pound skirt steak, in one piece and not tenderized
12 small corn or flour tortillas

directions

In a glass dish, combine all the ingredients except for the steak and tortillas, and mix well. Add the steak to the marinade, making sure the liquid coats the meat thoroughly. Cover the dish in plastic wrap and place in the refrigerator for 12 to 24 hours.

When ready to cook, drain the marinade from the meat and reserve.

Over hot coals, grill the steak until medium-rare, about 4-5 minutes per side, depending on the heat and distance from the coals. Let the meat rest 5 minutes while you prepare the sauce.

For the sauce, boil the reserved marinade in a small saucepan and reduce the liquid slightly. Adjust the seasoning, if necessary.

Slice the meat thinly against the grain. Warm the tortillas, add the steak and a drizzle of sauce, and adorn the tacos with other condiments you like, such as chopped cilantro, lime wedges and chopped onions.

pair with hawkes cabernet sauvignon

Hop Kiln Winery

6050 westside road, healdsburg, ca 95448
707-433-6491

www.hopkilnwinery.com

Born in Italy, Chef Renzo brings his cooking heritage and years of experience to Hop Kiln, where he oversees the winery's food and wine program. As our Maestro della Cucina, he cooks with a northern Italian accent, preparing classic dishes to pair with Hop Kiln and HK Generations wines. He bases his cooking on fresh ingredients and shops at local farms and farmers' markets, as he did at home in Italy. **Serves 4-6**

roasted pork sliders

with pickled red onions

chef Renzo Veronese

ingredients

Pork

3 bay leaves
1 tablespoon salt
1 tablespoon sugar
1 tablespoon Worcestershire sauce
10 dried juniper berries, crushed
1 gallon water
3 pounds pork shoulder
3 tablespoons Hop Kiln Yucatan Spice Rub
1 large onion, large dice
3 carrots, large dice
4 celery ribs, large dice
½ cup HK Generations Pinot Noir
1-½ cups water
7 ounces Hop Kiln Yucatan Spicy Sunset Barbeque Sauce
20 small dinner rolls, sliced in half and toasted

Pickled Red Onions

1 large red onion, thinly sliced
1 cup rice wine vinegar
1 cup distilled vinegar
1 tablespoon sugar
½ teaspoon red pepper flakes
2 cups water

directions

To prepare the pork, place the first 6 ingredients in a large pot and bring the mixture to a boil. Let the liquid cool, then add the pork shoulder. Refrigerate for a minimum of 2 hours, to allow the brine to soak into the meat.

Remove the pork from the brine and rub Hop Kiln Yucatan Spice Rub over the entire pork shoulder. Preheat the oven to 380°. In a large oven-proof pan, place the diced vegetables on the bottom, the pork shoulder on top, then pour the Pinot Noir and 1-½ cup water over all the ingredients. Cover the pan and roast the meat for approximately 2 hours.

When the pork is done, remove the pan from the oven. Discard the vegetables. Shred the pork with a fork while it's still warm, then mix in the barbeque sauce.

To prepare the pickled onions, put the sliced onion in a medium-sized bowl and set aside. Combine the rest of the ingredients in a saucepan and bring the mixture to a boil. Pour the hot mixture over the onions, cover the bowl loosely with foil, and refrigerate for a minimum of 2 hours.

To serve the sliders, place a spoonful of pork on the bottom half of a dinner roll, add a spoonful of pickled onions, and top with the other half of the dinner roll.

pair with hk generations pinot noir

Iron Horse Vineyards

9786 ross station road, sebastopol, ca 95472
707-887-1507

www.ironhorsevineyards.com

Chef Ruben's style is to prepare an outline of a menu ...
and then that morning, walk through the garden, picking
what's best and fresh and most flavorful to add in the
nuances. His food is intensely flavorful and satisfying,
and matches beautifully with our wines. **Serves 6**

roast pork

with hominy & garden tomatillo sauce
chef Ruben Gomez

ingredients

2-½ pounds pork shoulder, boneless and
cut into large fork-size chunks
olive oil as needed
3 bay leaves
1 quart fresh tomatillos
2-½ cups onions, large dice
1 cup garlic, whole
½ teaspoon whole clove
2 tablespoons whole coriander

1-½ tablespoons whole cumin
3 quarts roast chicken stock
2 cups roast poblano peppers, peeled and seeded
6-12 roast jalapeno peppers, peeled and seeded
3-6 roast Serrano peppers, peeled and seeded
2 cups hominy
3 tablespoons masa harina corn flour
½- ¾ cup lime juice
salt and pepper, to taste

directions preheat oven to 450°

Preheat a baking sheet pan in the oven. Place the pork in a large bowl and coat with a small amount of oil. Season with salt, pepper and 1 crushed bay leaf. Carefully arrange the pork evenly on the sheet pan; it may sizzle and spit, so be aware.

Roast the pork for 10-15 minutes, until it's golden brown on the contact side. With a wooden spoon, turn the pork and roast on all sides. While turning the pork, scrape loose any brown bits on the bottom of the pan. When the pork is evenly browned, remove it from oven and allow to cool.

In a large bowl, place the tomatillos, half of the onions, garlic, remaining 2 bay leaves, clove, coriander and cumin. Drizzle with oil and season with salt and pepper. Place the tomatillo mixture on a sheet pan and roast in the oven for 10 minutes, turning the vegetables while they become a golden brown. Remove the vegetables from the oven and allow them to cool.

Place the tomatillos, some of the peppers, and some chicken stock in a blender, filling the jar half way. Puree the mixture until smooth, set aside, and continue blending the remaining in batches. Reserve 1 quart of the stock.

In a large stock pot, place the remaining onions with a small amount of oil. Over a medium-high flame, sauté the onions until they begin to clear. Add the pork chunks, hominy and the pureed tomatillo sauce. Begin to add stock until a nice consistency is reached. The stew should be soupy and not too thick.

Bring the stew to a slow, steady boil. In a bowl, mix 1 cup of cold stock with the masa harina and stir into a lump-free slurry. When the stew begins to boil, add the masa mixture and stir until the slurry is dissolved. Let the stew simmer for 30 minutes or until the masa tastes cooked through. Add more masa or stock for the desired consistency. Finish seasoning with salt, pepper and lime juice to taste. Serve hot in warm bowls, with homemade tortillas on the side.

pair with iron horse pinot noir or sparkling wine

J. Keverson Winery

53 front street, healdsburg, ca 95448
707-433-3097

www.jkeverson.com

Our "Harvest Feast" tradition began a decade ago, when we decided that any great adventure deserves a great meal. Wanting to fully enjoy the fruits of our labors, we incorporate our J. Keverson Zinfandel into this fruit-infused roasted pork tenderloin. We like to serve it with roasted butternut squash soup, a multi-colored beet salad, and a yummy pear tart. **Serves 8**

entrées

zinfandel & cherry-infused
pork tenderloin

ingredients

2 pork tenderloins (1 pound each)
½ cup dried cranberries
¾ cup frozen sweet cherries (not sweetened)
½ cup J. Keverson Buck Hill Zinfandel
¼ cup balsamic vinegar
1 tablespoon blackberry honey
⅔ cup natural cranberry nectar (not artificially sweetened)
5 cloves garlic, minced
3 large shallots, minced
2 sprigs rosemary
1 tablespoon fresh rosemary, minced
2 tablespoons olive oil
sea salt and ground black pepper, to taste

directions

In a medium bowl, combine all the ingredients except the pork loins, salt and pepper. Stir well to blend.

Place the pork in a shallow glass baking dish and pour the marinade over. Cover the dish, put it in the refrigerator, and let the meat marinate several hours or overnight, turning the pork several times to keep all the surfaces moist.

Preheat the oven to 375°. Transfer the pork and marinade to a roasting pan and roast for 20-25 minutes. Several times during cooking, turn the meat and baste. Check for doneness with a meat thermometer—150°-155° for medium and 160° for medium-well.

When done, remove the pork loins from the oven. Remove the rosemary sprigs. Add salt and pepper to taste, cover the pan with foil, and allow the meat to rest for 5-10 minutes.

Place the pork loins on a cutting board and slice them ½-inch thick. Place the slices on a platter or individual plates, and spoon the sauce over the meat. Serve immediately.

pair with j. keverson zinfandel

J. Rickards Winery

24505 chianti road, cloverdale, ca 95425
707-758-3441

www.jrwinery.com

Petite Sirah is an essential ingredient in these braised short ribs, one of our favorite recipes. Wine dogs Kysha and Shelby love it, too, because they get the leftover bones. **Serves 6**

brown barn petite sirah-
braised short ribs

ingredients

4-5 pounds beef short ribs on the bone
salt and ground pepper, to taste
2 cups all-purpose flour
4 tablespoons olive oil, plus more if needed
2 large sweet yellow onions, chopped
4 large carrots, peeled and cut into 1-inch pieces
5 cloves garlic, chopped
1 bottle J. Rickards Brown Barn Petite Sirah
6 ounces tomato paste
4 fresh thyme sprigs
3 fresh rosemary sprigs
2 bay leaves
1 to 2 cups beef stock

directions preheat oven to 300°

Season the ribs with salt and pepper. Spread the flour on a baking sheet and dredge the ribs in the flour, coating well.

In a 5- to 6-quart Dutch oven, warm the 4 tablespoons of olive oil over medium-high heat, until the oil is near the smoking point. Brown the ribs on all sides, in batches if necessary, for about 10 minutes. Transfer the ribs to a large plate.

Add more oil, if needed, to the pot, then add the onions, carrots and garlic. Cook them over medium heat until just soft, about 10 minutes, and remove to another plate. Cover the plate with foil.

Add the Petite Sirah to the Dutch oven and stir to scrape up any browned bits. Add the tomato paste, thyme, rosemary and bay leaves and combine well. Increase the heat to medium-high and allow the mixture to reduce by half and thicken, 10-12 minutes. Add the ribs back to the Dutch oven, and add enough stock to come halfway up the sides of the ribs. Stir well, cover, and place the dish in the oven for 2-½ hours, stirring occasionally.

Add the vegetables to the Dutch oven and stir gently. Continue cooking the ribs another 1-½ hours or so; the dish is done when the meat is very tender. Remove the excess fat and the sprigs and bay leaves. Serve with noodles or mashed potatoes.

pair with j. rickards brown barn petite sirah

John Tyler Wines/Bacigalupi Vineyards

4375 westside road, healdsburg, ca 95448
707-473-0123

www.johntylerwines.com

As the family's third generation, twin sisters Nicole and Katie have just started to make their mark in the wine industry. Both have jumped in head first, co-marketing their family's first wine label: John Tyler Wines and Bacigalupi Vineyards. **Serves 12-15**

smoked pork cassoulet

chef Relish Culinary Adventures

ingredients

2 tablespoons pork fat (or bacon drippings)
1 large Spanish onion, small dice
2 celery ribs, small dice
1 large carrot, small dice
salt and pepper, to taste
1 head garlic, minced
1 tablespoon fresh thyme
1 tablespoon ground black pepper
3 tablespoons tomato paste
½ cup red wine
1-½ quarts pork stock (chicken stock is a good substitute)
1 bay leaf
2 smoked pork shanks (ham hocks)
4 cups cooked white Tepary beans
¼ cup parsley, chopped
2 cups fresh breadcrumbs
3 tablespoons butter, melted

directions preheat oven to 400°

In a heavy-bottom soup pot, melt the pork fat and add the onion, celery and carrot. Sauté the vegetables over medium heat until they're semi-soft and translucent, about 5 minutes. Add the garlic and a healthy pinch of salt, and cook the vegetables another minute or two, to incorporate the flavors.

Add the thyme, black pepper and tomato paste to the pot and cook, stirring constantly, until the paste takes on a rusty color. Add the wine and continue to cook until the liquid is reduced by ½. Add the stock, bay leaf and shanks to the pot and bring to a simmer. Simmer the pork for 30-45 minutes, remove it from the heat, and let it cool.

When the pork is cool enough to handle, remove the meat, chop it roughly and place it back in the liquid. Add the cooked beans to the pot and reduce, if necessary, to thicken. Remove the bay leaf and add the parsley. Check the pork and beans for seasoning, adding salt and/or pepper if necessary.

Grease a 3-quart casserole and add the pork and beans. Blend the butter with the breadcrumbs and sprinkle the mixture on top. Bake the cassoulet for 20-30 minutes, until the top is golden brown.

pair with john tyler bacigalupi vineyards zinfandel russian river valley

Korbel Champagne Cellars

13250 river road, guerneville, ca 95446
707-824-7000

www.korbel.com

Paella, with origins in Spain, is traditionally served in a large, shallow cast-iron skillet. A chafing dish can be used, and a large platter is nice to show how grand this dish truly is. **Serves 8-10**

entrées

wine country paella

chef Robin Lehnhoff-McCray

ingredients

3 cups basmati rice
3 tablespoons butter
2 teaspoons saffron threads
olive oil for sautéing
1 pound rock shrimp
1 pound mussels (optional)
2 tablespoons shallots, chopped
splash of white wine
1 cup onion, diced
2 tablespoons garlic, chopped
1 pound andouille sausage, sliced
1 pound chicken meat, cooked and diced
1 cup red bell pepper, diced
1 cup pasilla peppers, diced
2 jalapeno peppers, de-seeded and minced
3 cups canned diced tomatoes in juice
1 teaspoon saffron threads
½ cup fresh parsley, chopped
½ cup fresh oregano, chopped
salt and pepper, to taste

directions

Cook the rice in a pot of boiling water with the butter, saffron and a dash of salt. Cook until tender. Strain out the water (like when cooking pasta). Pour the saffron rice into a large bowl that can accommodate all the other ingredients. Set aside.

In a sauté pan, heat a teaspoon of olive oil and sauté the rock shrimp just until they're done, and set aside. In the same pan, sauté the mussels and shallots in olive oil, until the mussels are warm. Add a splash of your favorite white wine and cover the pan to finish cooking. The mussels are cooked when they pop open; discard those that don't. Remove them from the heat immediately, and set aside.

In a separate pan, sauté the onion and garlic and let them sweat. Add the sausage, chicken, peppers and canned tomatoes and juice. Let simmer for 10 minutes.

Add 1 more teaspoon of saffron to this and let simmer for 15 more minutes, to blend the flavors. Add the cooked seafood and fresh herbs, and season with salt and pepper. Pour the mixture into the saffron rice and combine. Reheat in a 425° oven for 15 minutes, uncovered, and serve.

pair with korbel brut or chardonnay champagne

Locals Tasting Room

21023-a geyserville avenue, geyserville, ca 95441
707-857-4900

www.tastelocalwines.com

Diavola chef/owner Dino Bugica practices the time-honored tradition of cucina povera—combining the most basic, locally available ingredients with recipes that have endured through centuries. This dish, *spezzatino d' agnello alle olive* in Italian, is classic cucina povera. If artichokes aren't in season, substitute with any hearty vegetables in season. **Serves 10**

entrées

braised lamb stew

with citrus-marinated olives & artichokes

chef Dino Bugica, Chef / Owner, Diavola Restaurant

ingredients

Olives

1 cup oil-cured black olives, pitted
2 cloves garlic, minced
zest of 1 lemon
2-3 bay leaves
3–4 tablespoons extra virgin olive oil

Lamb

4 tablespoons olive oil, or as needed
3 pounds boneless lamb shoulder, trimmed of excess
fat and cut into 2-inch pieces
salt and freshly ground pepper
3 yellow onions, sliced
pinch ground cinnamon
2 cups meat stock, or as needed
½ cup dry white wine (optional)
1 tablespoon fresh rosemary or 2 tablespoons fresh
marjoram, chopped
fresh lemon juice (optional)
12 baby artichokes, cleaned, with chokes removed

directions

To prepare the olives, combine them in a small sauté pan with the garlic, lemon zest, bay leaves and olive oil. Warm the mixture gently over low heat. Remove the pan from the heat, let the olives cool, then transfer them to a covered container. Marinate the olives at least overnight and up to 3 days in the refrigerator.

To prepare the lamb, place a large sauté pan over high heat and coat the bottom with 2 tablespoons of olive oil. Working in batches, add the lamb pieces and brown them on all sides, adding oil as needed and seasoning with salt and pepper as you turn the meat. Each batch should take 8-10 minutes. As each batch is ready, use a slotted spoon to transfer it to a Dutch oven or other heavy pot.

Return the sauté pan to medium heat and add the onions to the fat remaining in the pan. Sprinkle them with the cinnamon and sauté until softened, about 8 minutes. Add the onions to the lamb in the Dutch oven. Pour ½ cup of the stock and the wine into the sauté pan to deglaze it over medium-high heat, scraping up all the brown bits. Add the scrapings to the lamb.

Add the rosemary or marjoram and the remaining 1-½ cups of stock to the lamb, or as needed just to cover the meat. Bring the lamb to a gentle boil over medium-high heat, then reduce the heat to low, cover, and simmer for 1-½ hours. Add the olives and artichokes, re-cover the pot, and continue to simmer until the meat is tender, about 25 minutes longer.

Taste and adjust the seasoning. Add a little lemon juice, if needed, to temper the richness, and serve the lamb over polenta.

pair with syrah or petite sirah

Longboard Vineyards

5 fitch street, healdsburg, ca 95448
707-433-3473

www.longboardvineyards.com

We know what you're thinking...
"What does surfing have to do with wine?"
Try balance, harmony and nature for starters.
Longboard was born from the passion of Oded
Shakked: surfer first, winemaker later, who brings a
unique perspective to winegrowing. **Serves 8**

entrées

gumbo

with duck, ham & sausage

chef Mike Matson, Vintage Valley Catering

ingredients

1 bottle Longboard Dakine Syrah
3 gallons brown chicken stock
2 cups tomatoes, diced
½ cup filé powder
3 cups flour
3 cups peanut oil
2 cups celery, diced
2 cups okra, sliced
2 cups yellow onion, diced
2 cups red bell pepper, diced
1 cup yellow bell pepper, diced
3 andouille sausages, diced
4 braised duck legs, diced
2 braised ham hocks, diced
2 cups white rice, cooked
Creole seasoning, to taste
lemon juice, to taste
salt and pepper, to taste

directions braise the sausages, ham hocks and duck legs before starting the recipe

In a large stock pot, add the Syrah and simmer the wine until it is reduced by ⅔. Add the chicken stock and cook until the liquid is reduced by ½. Add the tomatoes and filé powder, and continue to simmer.

Meanwhile, prepare a roux by browning the flour and peanut oil in a Dutch oven. Cook the mixture on medium heat, stirring constantly, for ½ hour. Don't allow the roux to scorch or burn. When the roux is dark brown, carefully add it to the simmering stock. Cook for 10 minutes, then strain the liquid into another pot.

In a non-stick skillet, sweat the celery, okra, onions and peppers, and add them to the strained stock. Add the diced meats and rice. Add Creole seasoning and lemon juice to taste, and cook through, adding salt and pepper, if necessary.

pair with longboard dakine syrah

Moshin Vineyards

10295 westside road, healdsburg, ca 95448
707-433-5499

www.moshinvineyards.com

We're Pinot Noir enthusiasts, and what better way to celebrate our enthusiasm than to pair our favorite wine with wild mushrooms? This dish is comfort food, emphasizing the tastes of the earth: filling and savory, heady and aromatic, seemingly decadent, yet casual enough for a weekday meal. **Serves 6**

wild mushrooms
on soft polenta

chef Dan Lucia

ingredients

Mushrooms

6 tablespoons olive oil
5 pounds mixed wild mushrooms, sliced
(if not in season, use farmed Gourmet Mushrooms)
3 tablespoons butter
1 yellow onion, diced
1 red onion, diced
1 fennel bulb, sliced
½ cup Moshin Sauvignon Blanc
½ cup vegetable or mushroom stock
1 cup heavy cream
2 bunches baby spinach, rough chopped
3 tablespoons fresh thyme, coarsely chopped
salt and pepper, to taste

Polenta

2 cups vegetable stock
2 cups half and half
4 cloves garlic, minced
1 cup polenta
½ cup butter
1 cup Parmigiano-Reggiano cheese, grated
salt and pepper, to taste

directions

To prepare the mushrooms, in a stock pot, heat the oil and add the sliced mushrooms. Sauté until the mushrooms are lightly browned, approximately 10 minutes. Remove the mushrooms from the pot and set aside.

In the same pot, add the butter, onions and fennel, and sauté until the onions are translucent. Add the Sauvignon Blanc and continue to cook until the liquid is reduced by half. Add the stock and heavy cream, and bring to a simmer.

Add the spinach, sautéed mushrooms and thyme. Continue to simmer until the spinach is completely wilted. Season with salt and pepper.

To prepare the polenta, in a small stock pot, bring the vegetable stock and the half and half to a simmer. Add the garlic and polenta, bring the mixture back to a simmer, and stir continuously with a whisk, for approximately 15-20 minutes. Add the butter, salt and pepper. The polenta should have a very smooth consistency; if it becomes too thick, add more stock. Add the grated cheese and stir until it's completely melted.

To serve, scoop the polenta in a large serving bowl and ladle on the mushrooms sauce.

pair with moshin vineyards pinot noir

Papapietro Perry Winery

4791 dry creek road, healdsburg, ca 95448
707-433-0422

www.papapietro-perry.com

Have a favorite recipe to pair with our Pinot Noir or Zinfandel?
We would love to post it on our online recipe page. Send
us an email at info@papapietro-perry.com with the recipe
and the Papapietro Perry wine that you pair it with, and
we'll post it and give you credit for the recipe. **Serves 8**

coq au vin

papapietro perry style

chef Bruce Riezenman, Park Avenue Catering

ingredients

32 pearl onions, peeled
1 teaspoon sugar
1-½ ounces water
2 frying chickens, 3-½ pounds each, cut into 8 pieces
salt and pepper, to taste
1 tablespoon canola oil
1 teaspoon butter
¼ pound bacon, sliced and cut into ½-inch pieces
1 medium red onion, diced
3 carrots, peeled and sliced thinly
4 celery stalks, peeled and sliced

4 bay leaves
1 teaspoon thyme
1 teaspoon rosemary
½ teaspoon oregano
1-½ pounds button mushrooms, quartered
3 cups Papapietro Perry Pinot Noir
2 cups beef broth
2 cups chicken broth
1 tablespoon cornstarch
½ pound bacon, sliced, baked crisp in the oven, and crumbled

directions preheat oven to 325°

Place the pearl onions in a small sauce pot with the sugar and water. Boil slowly until the onions are tender. Allow the liquid to evaporate, and continue to cook on medium heat until the sugar turns golden and coats the onions. Remove the onions from the pan and set aside.

Season the chicken with salt and pepper. Place a shallow, heavy-bottomed pot over medium-high heat. Add the oil and allow it to heat until you see ripples on the surface when you swirl the pan. Add the butter, swirl the pan once, and place each piece of chicken in the pot, skin-side down. Cook until the chicken is golden brown, about 5 minutes. Flip the chicken, lower the heat to medium, and cook on the other side for 3 minutes. Remove the chicken from the pot and set aside.

Add the bacon to the pot, and cook until it gets crispy and brown, about 5 minutes. Add the red onions, then cover and cook until the onions are soft, about 5 minutes. Add the celery, carrots and herbs. Cover and cook for 5 minutes more. Add the mushrooms and increase the heat to high. Cook until the vegetable mixture is dry.

Add the Pinot Noir to the vegetables, and boil until the wine has been reduced by half. Add the beef and chicken broths and bring to a boil again. Season the mixture lightly with salt and pepper. Add the chicken pieces and return to a simmer. Cover and bake in the oven for 45 minutes, or until the chicken is tender.

Remove the pot from the oven, remove the lid, and allow the dish to cool for 15 minutes. Remove the chicken from the pot, place it in a glass dish and cover with foil. Turn off the oven and place the covered chicken in the oven to remain warm.

Remove as much fat as you can from the top of the cooking liquid. Put the pot back on the heat and reduce it by half. Add salt and pepper if needed.

In a small bowl, mix the cornstarch with 1 tablespoon of Pinot Noir, and stir to make a smooth slurry. Add the cornstarch slowly to the simmering sauce, adding just enough to thicken the sauce so that so it coats a spoon. Simmer for 5 minutes.

To serve, pour the sauce over the warm chicken, and garnish with the crumbled bacon and the pearl onions.

pair with papapietro perry pinot noir

Ridge Vineyards Lytton Springs

650 lytton springs road, healdsburg, ca 95448
707-433-7721

www.ridgewine.com

These meatballs go perfectly with the spicy Zinfandels from Ridge Vineyards. The dried currants and toasted pine nuts add an unexpected twist to traditional spaghetti and meatballs. **Serves 4-6**

sicilian meatballs

with spaghetti

ingredients

1-½ quarts tomato sauce
²/₃ cup fresh breadcrumbs
3 tablespoons milk
⅓ cup Parmesan cheese, grated
¼ cup yellow onion, finely chopped
3 tablespoons fresh basil, chopped
1 large egg
1 garlic clove, minced
¼ teaspoon black pepper, ground
1 pound sweet Italian sausage, bulk or casings removed
2 tablespoons pine nuts, toasted
2 tablespoons dried currants
1 pound spaghetti
Parmesan cheese for grating

directions preheat oven to 350°

Gently heat the tomato sauce in a large pot on the stove.

Lightly oil a baking sheet. In a medium-sized bowl, mix the bread crumbs and milk, and let stand for 5 minutes. Mix in the Parmesan, onion, basil, egg, garlic and pepper. Add the sausage, pine nuts and currants, and blend well.

Using wet hands, form the mixture into 1-¼-inch balls. Place the meatballs on the oiled baking sheet, and bake until they're light brown and cooked through, about 30 minutes. Add the meatballs to the heated tomato sauce.

Cook the spaghetti in a large pot of boiling salted water. When it's just tender but still firm to the bite, remove the pasta from the heat and drain. Mound the spaghetti in a warmed dish. Bring the sauce and meatballs to a simmer. Spoon the meatballs and sauce over the spaghetti. If desired, grate Parmesan cheese over the sauce.

pair with ridge zinfandel

Rodney Strong Vineyards

11455 old redwood highway, healdsburg, ca 95448
707-431-1533

www.rodneystrong.com

Susan and I love traveling in the South, especially in and around New Orleans. We're always searching out the best red beans and rice we can find. For this version of cassoulet, we use our favorite Southern ingredients. This dish is always best when made a day ahead of time. **Serves 4**

entrées

red bean 'cassoulet'

with crispy duck, ham hock & andouille sausage

chef Jeff Mall, Chef / Owner, Zin Restaurant & Wine Bar

ingredients

4 duck confit legs, store-bought and already prepared
1 ham hock
6 cups chicken stock
1 pound dried light red kidney beans, rinsed and picked over
3 slices bacon, diced
1 andouille sausage, diced
1 red bell pepper, medium dice
1 green pepper, medium dice
4 green onions, sliced
3 cloves garlic, sliced thin

½ bunch Italian parsley, chopped
1 teaspoon cayenne pepper
¼ teaspoon crushed red pepper flakes
1 bay leaf
2 teaspoons fresh thyme, minced
salt and pepper, to taste
¾ cup fresh bread crumbs
½ cup Parmesan cheese, grated
3 tablespoons parsley, chopped
2 tablespoons olive oil
dry rub seasoning of your choice

directions start this recipe 1 day ahead

In a large pot, simmer the ham hock in the chicken stock for 1 hour. Add the beans, bacon, sausage, peppers, onions, garlic, parsley, cayenne, red pepper flakes, bay leaf and thyme, bring the mixture to a boil, then reduce the heat to low and simmer for 2 hours. Season to taste with salt and pepper. Chill overnight.

Combine the bread crumbs, Parmesan cheese, remaining parsley and olive oil in a food processor. Pulse to combine.

Place the confit duck legs in an oven-proof roasting dish and sprinkle them with the dry rub. Divide the red bean mixture into individual, oven-proof ramekins and top them with the bread crumb mixture.

Place the duck legs and the bean-filled ramekins in a preheated 350° oven for 20 to 25 minutes. The duck legs should be brown and crispy, the bean casseroles golden brown on top and bubbling below.

To serve, place 1 duck leg on top of each ramekin.

pair with rodney strong vineyards symmetry red meritage

Route 128 Vineyards & Winery

21079 geyserville avenue, geyserville, ca 95441
707-696-0004

www.route128winery.com

The beans can be prepared 1 to 3 days in
advance, cutting down the preparation time on
the day you serve this hearty dish. **Serves 6**

entrées

braised pork shoulder

over spanish beans

chef Rian Rinn

ingredients

Beans

3 cups dried white beans
1 onion, quartered
1 carrot, quartered
sprig of thyme
2 garlic cloves
1 bay leaf
2 whole cloves
$1/8$ cup olive oil
2 shallots, diced
$1/2$ cup parsley, chopped

Pork Shoulder

$1/4$ cup peanut or vegetable oil
2-$1/2$ pounds pork shoulder, cut into 2-$1/2$- inch cubes, equaling 12 pieces
3 onions, thinly sliced
6 garlic cloves, crushed
3 teaspoons tomato paste
$1/2$ bottle Route 128 Syrah
2 quarts chicken stock
1 teaspoon chili flakes
1 tablespoon unsweetened cocoa powder
6 teaspoons fresh thyme
2 sprigs rosemary
$1/8$ teaspoon dried lavender
3 tablespoons honey
3 tablespoons sherry vinegar
salt and pepper, to taste
lemon zest and sea salt, for garnish

directions

To prepare the beans, place the first 7 ingredients in a stock pot and cover with water, 3 level fingers above the surface of the beans. Cook on low for 1-$1/2$ to 3 hours, adding liquid, if necessary, during the cooking time. When done, the beans should be soft, not mushy. Remove them from the heat, drain, and discard the vegetables.

To prepare the pork, heat the oil in a large roasting pan. Season the pork with salt, place it in the pan and sear the meat until it's golden brown on all sides. Remove the pork from the pan.

Drain off $2/3$ of the oil from the roasting pan. Add the onions, garlic and tomato paste, and sauté until the onions are translucent and the paste is slightly brown. Put the pork back in the pan and cover it with the onions.

Preheat the oven to 375°. Add the wine to the pan and cook the pork mixture in the oven until the wine is reduced by half, about 25 minutes. Remove the pan from the oven, add the chicken stock, chili flakes and cocoa powder, and return the pan to the oven. Bake the pork, basting frequently, until $2/3$ of the liquid is gone, about 1 hour.

Add the thyme, rosemary, lavender, honey and sherry vinegar. Incorporate them into the existing liquid. Keep the mixture warm in the oven.

To finish the beans, heat $1/8$ cup olive oil in a pan and add 2 diced shallots. Sauté them until the shallots just start to turn brown. Add the prepared beans and salt, if necessary. Stir until the beans begin to turn white around the edges and start to crisp. Add $1/2$ cup chopped parsley and stir.

To serve, divide the beans among 6 plates. Remove the meat from the oven and baste with the pan liquids. Place 2 pieces of pork on each plate over the beans. Drizzle the pan sauces over the top, and garnish with lemon zest and sea salt to taste.

pair with route 128 syrah

Simi Winery

16275 healdsburg avenue, healdsburg, ca 95448
707-433-6981

www.simiwinery.com

Simi Winery continues its century-old tradition of sharing a passion for wine and food with guests who visit our historic winery in Healdsburg. Chef Eric Lee creates wine country cuisine to complement the exceptional wines of our winemakers. We hope you enjoy this creamy polenta topped with lamb meatballs. **Serves 4**

entrées

lamb & herb meatballs

with creamy polenta

chef Eric Lee

ingredients

Meatballs

1 pound ground lamb
½ pound ground beef, pork or Italian sausage
2 large eggs, beaten
1 cup fresh breadcrumbs
1 tablespoon garlic, minced
¼ cup Italian flat parsley, chopped
½ cup Parmigiano-Reggiano cheese, grated
1-½ teaspoons salt
1 teaspoon freshly ground black pepper
1 teaspoon fresh basil, chopped
1 teaspoon fresh mint, chopped
1 teaspoon fresh oregano, chopped
¼ cup olive oil for frying

Tomato Sauce

2 tablespoons olive oil
1 cup onion, chopped
1 tablespoon garlic, minced
1 cup Simi Zinfandel
1 cup chicken or veal stock
3 cups crushed, fire-roasted tomatoes
1 tablespoon fresh basil, chopped
salt and pepper, to taste

Polenta

4 cups water
1 tablespoon salt
1 cup polenta
2 tablespoons unsalted butter
¼ cup Parmigiano-Reggiano cheese, grated
salt and pepper, to taste

directions

To prepare the meatballs, mix everything together very well in a large bowl. Form the mixture into balls and refrigerate, covered. Heat a large saucepan over medium heat. Add some olive oil and fry the meatballs on all sides, until they're golden brown. Turn the meatballs only when a side is completely golden; they will stick if you move them too soon. Set aside.

To make the sauce, pour out the remaining oil from the pan used to cook the meatballs. Over medium heat, add the olive oil to the pan. Add the onions and cook for 2 minutes, or until golden. Add the garlic and cook for 1 minute. Add the wine and reduce the liquid by half. Add the stock and crushed tomatoes. Season with salt and pepper and bring to a simmer. Add the meatballs to the pan, and cook over low heat for 30 minutes. Add the basil, and season with salt and pepper.

To prepare the polenta, bring the water and salt to a boil in a medium saucepan. Slowly add the polenta into the water, whisking constantly. Bring the mixture to a boil, stir, reduce the heat to low and cover with a lid. Whisk the polenta every 5 minutes. After 30 minutes, add the butter and the cheese. Season with salt and pepper, if needed. Cover and keep warm.

To serve, spoon some polenta onto a plate and top with some of the sauce and meatballs. Sprinkle with chopped basil, parsley, mint and grated Parmigiano-Reggiano.

pair with simi dry creek valley zinfandel

Suncé Winery & Vineyard

1839 olivet road, santa rosa, ca 95401
707-526-9463

www.suncewinery.com

Take the usual French coq au vin ingredients of chicken,
vegetables and red wine, and corrupt them the Sicilian way, with
loads of garlic, tomatoes and Italian sausage, as we do. **Serves 8**

entrées

coq au vin

alla italiana

chef Janae Franicevic

ingredients

Coq au Vin

2 tablespoons vegetable oil
5 cloves garlic, crushed
½ cup all-purpose flour
1 teaspoon poultry seasoning
4 pounds dark-meat chicken pieces
4 links sweet Italian sausage, sliced
1 cup onion, chopped
3 carrots, sliced
½ pound fresh mushrooms, sliced
½ teaspoon dried rosemary
1 cup Sunce Zora's Estate Pinot Noir
1 14.5-ounce can whole peeled tomatoes
salt and pepper to taste

Creamy Polenta

3 cups water
1 cup milk
1 cup medium-grain yellow polenta
salt to taste
1 cup milk
5 tablespoons butter
1 cup cream cheese

directions

To prepare the coq au vin, in a large skillet, heat the oil. Add ½ of the garlic. Season the flour with poultry seasoning. Roll the chicken pieces in the flour, then brown them in the skillet for 4 or 5 minutes. Add the sausage and sauté for a few minutes. Add the onion, carrots, mushrooms, rosemary and the remaining garlic, and mix well.

Add the wine and tomatoes, and stir. Cover the skillet and let the mixture simmer over low heat for 25 minutes. Season with salt and pepper to taste, and simmer for another 20 minutes. Let the chicken cool, covered, for 10 minutes before serving with the polenta.

To prepare the polenta, place the water in a stock pot and season it lightly with salt. Bring the water to a boil over high heat, then add the milk, and quickly whisk in the polenta until it is fully incorporated. Reduce the heat to a low simmer, add the butter and allow the polenta to cook, stirring occasionally, for 30 minutes. Finish by stirring in the cream cheese and salt, to taste.

pair with sunce zemlja's blend

Twomey Cellars

3000 westside road, healdsburg, ca 95448
800-505-4850

www.twomeycellars.com

At the winery, we slow-cook this dish in our wood-burning oven. We burn old barrel staves that impart a caramelized, grapey-like smoke flavor to foods. If you have trouble finding fresh pork shank, you can use pork shoulder or smoked ham hocks. If you use ham hocks, omit the pancetta from the recipe. **Serves 8**

entrées

braised pork shanks

osso bucco

chef Dominic Orsini, Twomey Cellars & Silver Oak

ingredients

Pork Shanks

6 fresh pork shanks
¼ cup olive oil
salt and pepper, to taste
8 ounces pancetta, large dice
2 yellow onions, peeled and quartered
1 carrot, peeled and quartered
1 celery stalk, quartered
2 bay leaves
3 tablespoons juniper berries, crushed
1 cup Twomey Pinot Noir
2 cups crushed tomatoes
4 cups chicken stock

Polenta

4 cups whole milk
1 cup polenta
1 bay leaf
1 tablespoon salt
1 small butternut squash, roasted, peeled and pureed
½ cup Parmesan cheese, grated

Gremolata

1 red onion, sliced thin and soaked overnight in rice wine vinegar
1 zest of fresh orange
¼ cup parsley, chopped
4 garlic cloves, sliced thin
24 Castelvetrano olives, pitted and chopped lightly
¼ cup high-quality extra virgin olive oil

directions preheat oven to 500°

To prepare the pork shanks, coat them with olive oil and season them with salt and pepper. Place the shanks into a roasting pan and then into the oven for 15 minutes, to "oven-sear" the meat. Be sure to give the pan a quarter turn every 5 minutes. After the first 10 minutes, add the pancetta to the pan to sear, as well.

Once the shanks are golden brown on all sides, add the onions, celery, carrot, bay leaves and juniper berries. Turn the oven down to 300° and let the meat cook an additional 10 minutes.

Remove the pan from the oven and place it on a large burner on high heat. Add the Pinot Noir, tomatoes and chicken broth, and bring to a simmer. Cover with a lid or foil and place the pan back into the oven, cooking for 90 minutes or so, until the shanks are tender enough to cut with a fork.

Remove the shanks from the pan and reserve the liquid. Strain the vegetables out of the broth and return the liquid to the roasting pan. Boil until half of the liquid is cooked away. Return the shanks to the liquid.

To prepare the polenta, bring the milk, bay leaf and salt to a boil. Gently sprinkle in the polenta, stirring the entire time. Continue to stir until the polenta re-boils, then turn the heat to low and add the Parmesan. Cook, stirring frequently, for an additional 10 minutes.

To prepare the gremolata, in a small bowl, mix together the pickled red onions, orange zest, parsley, garlic, olives and olive oil.

To assemble the dish, on a large serving platter or individual plates, pour some polenta, place the braised shanks on top, and ladle the broth over the shanks. Drizzle with the gremolata and serve.

pair with twomey russian river valley pinot noir

White Oak Vineyards & Winery

7505 highway 128, healdsburg, ca 95448
707-433-8429

www.whiteoakwinery.com

Dan Lucia, contributing chef for White Oak Vineyards & Winery, created this recipe to complement our 2008 Russian River Valley Sauvignon Blanc. Delicious and comforting, it can be served as an entrée, appetizer, or for brunch. White Oak owner Bill Myers loves this dish because it's filling enough to satisfy his appetite, and reminds him of carefree days catching wild shrimp in Alaska. **Serves 8**

rock shrimp

with wilted greens & polenta

chef Dan Lucia

ingredients

Polenta

4 cups milk
4 cups chicken stock (can substitute with water)
2 cups polenta
10 cloves garlic, chopped
1 cup aged white cheddar cheese, grated
salt and pepper, to taste

Rock Shrimp with Wilted Greens

4 tablespoons olive oil
2 shallots, chopped
8 cloves garlic, chopped
3 pounds rock shrimp
1 cup Wild Oak Sauvignon Blanc
½ cup butter
1 bunch baby arugula, roughly chopped
1 bunch baby spinach, roughly chopped
1 bunch swiss chard, roughly chopped
salt and pepper, to taste

directions

For the polenta, in a stock pot, bring the milk and chicken stock to a simmer. Add the polenta and garlic. Turn the heat down as low as possible and slowly let the polenta cook, stirring it until it's smooth and creamy, approximately 25 minutes.

While frequently stirring the polenta, prepare the rock shrimp and wilted greens. In a large sauté pan, heat the olive oil. Add the shallots and garlic, and sauté for 3 minutes.

Add the rock shrimp and continue to sauté, stirring with a wooden spoon for approximately 5 minutes. Add the Sauvignon Blanc and cook until the wine has been reduced by half. Add the butter and stir until it melts. Add the greens and cook until they are completely wilted. Season with salt and pepper.

Just before serving, add the cheese, salt and pepper to the polenta and stir to combine. Spoon the polenta into bowls, and top with the rock shrimp and greens.

pair with white oak sauvignon blanc

desserts
& sweets

Camellia Inn

211 north street, healdsburg, ca 95448
707-433-8182

www.camelliainn.com

When we held our first winter Robert Burns Supper at the inn, my mom, Del, wanted to make a contribution to the evening (Robert Burns is the Scottish poet who wrote "Auld Lang Syne"). With Mom's inspiration, every year we turn our parlor into a grand banquet hall and enjoy an evening of poetry, song and a Scottish meal that includes the mysterious and tasty haggis. For dessert, we have a traditional layered trifle and this delicious pecan whiskey cake, adapted from a recipe published in Bon Appétit magazine in 1982. **Serves 14-20**

desserts & sweets

pecan whiskey cake

chef Lucy Lewand, Innkeeper

ingredients

Cake
1 cup sweet butter (unsalted)
2 cups granulated sugar
6 eggs, room temperature, yolks and whites separated
3-½ cups cake flour
4 teaspoons baking powder
2 teaspoons ground nutmeg
1 teaspoon salt
1 cup bourbon or whiskey
½ cup all-purpose flour
4 cups pecan halves
3 cups golden raisins

Sauce
1 cup light brown sugar
1 cup butter
½ cup whipping cream

directions preheat oven to 325°

Grease and flour 2 small bundt pans. Cream the butter and sugar. Add the egg yolks, 1 at a time, to the butter/sugar mixture and combine.

Sift together the cake flour, sugar, baking powder, nutmeg and salt. Add the dry ingredients to the butter and sugar in 4 batches, alternating with ¼ cup of whiskey.

Combine the ½ cup of all-purpose flour with the pecans and raisins, and stir them into the cake batter. Beat the egg whites until stiff. Fold half of the egg whites into the batter, then gently fold in the remaining half. Spoon the batter into the prepared bundt pans and bake for about 1 hour. Let the cake cool in the pan for 10 minutes, and turn it out.

For the sauce, combine all the ingredients in a heavy saucepan and cook over low heat, until the sugar is dissolved. Remove the pan from the heat, and whisk the sauce for 1 minute.

Serve the cake in thin slices with the sauce and additional whipped cream, if desired.

pair with a sonoma county port-style wine

Fritz Underground Winery

24691 dutcher creek road, cloverdale, ca 95425
707-894-3389

www.fritzwinery.com

Rich, not-too-sweet dark chocolate is ideal for matching with our Late Harvest Zinfandel. Adding fleur de sel (gourmet sea salt) brings out a new depth of flavor in the chocolate, and makes for a more complex synergy with the wine. Start the recipe one day in advance of serving. **Makes 16 pieces**

desserts & sweets

late harvest zinfandel

dark chocolates with fleur de sel

chef Julie Herson

ingredients

16 ounces premium dark chocolate, chopped
¾ cup Fritz Late Harvest Zinfandel
¼ cup heavy whipping cream
fleur de sel, or any large-flaked sea salt
8 ounces premium dark chocolate, chopped

directions

Combine the 16 ounces of chocolate, wine and cream in a double boiler and heat on low, allowing the chocolate to melt slowly. Stir gently yet constantly, until the mixture is smooth.

Remove the mixture from the heat and pour it into an 8-inch by 4-inch loaf pan lined with waxed paper. Refrigerate overnight.

The next day, unmold the chocolate from the pan and slice it into equal-sized squares with a hot knife. Set the squares aside on a waxed-paper-lined tray.

Meanwhile, gently melt the 8-ounce batch of chocolate over a double boiler. Dip each chocolate square into the melted chocolate, using a fork to lift each piece out, and place them on a lined tray. Garnish each square with a flake or two of fleur de sel on top, and allow the chocolate to set in the refrigerator before serving.

pair with fritz late harvest zinfandel

Geyser Peak Winery

22281 chianti road, geyserville, ca 95441
707-857-9400

www.geyserpeakwinery.com

The perfect ending to a casual fall meal is a decadent chocolate or two. Port is a traditional wine to pair with chocolate, yet Cabernet Sauvignon works nicely, especially when the chocolates have Cabernet in them, as these do. **Makes 50 chocolate cups**

desserts & sweets

chocolate-cabernet ganache

chef Bruce Riezenman, Park Avenue Catering

ingredients

²/₃ cup heavy whipping cream
2 teaspoons dark-roast coffee, ground fine
½ cup light corn syrup
3 tablespoons blackstrap molasses
4-½ ounces milk chocolate, chopped
5 ounces bittersweet (dark) chocolate, chopped
½ cup Geyser Peak Walking Tree Cabernet Sauvignon, reduced to 1 tablespoon
50 pre-made chocolate cups
cocoa nibs for garnish

directions

In a saucepan, bring the cream just to a simmer and remove the pan from the heat. Add the ground coffee to the cream, stir, and let it sit for 10 minutes. Add the molasses and corn syrup to the cream and mix thoroughly.

Meanwhile, place the milk and bittersweet chocolates in a small mixing bowl and place it over a pot of boiling water, making sure the bottom of the bowl does not touch the water. Allow the chocolate to melt, add it to the warm cream mixture, and mix until it's smooth. It may be necessary to place the mixture in a food processor to make sure it is smooth. Once the mixture is smooth, add the reduced wine.

While the chocolate mixture is still slightly warm and runny, pour it into the pre-made chocolate cups; if the mixture is too hot, it will melt the cups. Sprinkle the cups with cocoa nibs and allow them to set for at least 2 hours or overnight.

pair with geyser peak walking tree cabernet sauvignon

Highlands Resort

14000 woodland drive, guerneville, ca 95446
707-869-0333

www.highlandsresort.com

Guests willing to pick wild blackberries in our back meadow get fresh berry cobbler for breakfast the next day. (Mom claims ice cream makes it a balanced breakfast – fruit, grains and dairy!) Willing guests get the "blackberry picking kit" – a small bucket with a neck strap, which frees hands for picking and holding thorns out of the way, a larger bowl, and advice NOT to wear designer clothing. The first serving of cobbler the next morning goes to the top blackberry picker. **Serves 4-6**

desserts & sweets

blackberry cobbler

chef Lynette McLean, Innkeeper

ingredients

1 quart fresh blackberries
¼ cup plus ½ cup sugar
1 tablespoon quick-cooking tapioca (optional)
1/3 cup whole milk
1 egg, beaten
1-½ cups all-purpose flour
2 teaspoons baking powder
½ teaspoon salt
¼ cup butter, chilled
vanilla ice cream (optional)

directions preheat oven to 450°

Spray a 9-inch by 9-inch baking dish with non-stick spray. Rinse and drain the berries, and place them in the dish. Sprinkle the berries with up to ¼ cup of sugar to adjust the sweetness, if needed. Sprinkle with the tapioca, if using, to thicken the cobbler.

In a small bowl, mix together the milk and egg. Set aside.

In a medium bowl, add the flour, baking powder, salt and ½ cup of sugar. Mix well. Cut in the chilled butter with a pastry cutter, or use your fingers to press the butter into the dry ingredients, until the lumps of butter are no larger than small peas.

Add the milk and egg mix to the flour mixture, stirring just enough to moisten; don't over-mix. Drop spoonfuls of the batter onto the berries, until all the batter is gone.

Bake the cobbler for 15 minutes at 450°, then turn the oven down to 350° and bake 30 minutes more. The cobbler is done when the top is golden brown and the berries are bubbling in the center of the dish.

Cool slightly before serving with a scoop of vanilla ice cream.

The Honor Mansion

14891 grove street, healdsburg, ca 95448
707-433-4277

www.honormansion.com

Biscotti are twice-baked, low-moisture cookies that are great for dunking into coffee after dinner. We dip our lemon biscotti in creamy white chocolate before serving them to our guests, transforming a light dessert into a decadent one. **Makes 40 cookies**

desserts & sweets

lemon biscotti

chef Cathi Fowler, Innkeeper

ingredients

²/₃ cup sugar
½ cup vegetable oil
1 tablespoon lemon peel, grated
1-½ teaspoons lemon extract or lemon oil
2 eggs
2-½ cups flour
1 teaspoon baking powder
¼ teaspoon baking soda
½ cup almonds, slivered
½ cup white chocolate chips

directions preheat oven to 350°

In a large bowl, mix the sugar, vegetable oil, lemon peel, lemon extract/oil and eggs. Stir in the flour, baking powder, baking soda and almonds.

On a lightly floured surface, knead the dough until it's smooth. On an ungreased cookie sheet, shape the dough into 2 rectangles, 10 by 3 inches each, and bake for 25-30 minutes, or until a toothpick inserted in the center of the dough comes out clean. Allow to cool on the cookie sheet for 15 minutes.

Cut the biscotti crosswise into ½-inch slices. Place the slices, cut side down, on a baking sheet, and bake about 15 minutes more, turning once, until the cookies are crisp and lightly browned. Remove the biscotti from the tray and allow them to cool completely.

In a small saucepan, melt the white chocolate chips. Dip one end of each biscotti into the melted chocolate, and place on a cooling rack to dry before serving.

Mill Creek Vineyards

1401 westside road, healdsburg, ca 95448
707-431-2121

www.millcreekwinery.com

Chocolate lovers get their fix three ways in this
sinfully rich cheesecake. The secret weapon:
Mill Creek's own Chocolate Cabernet Sauce. **Serves 12**

desserts & sweets

triple
chocolate cheesecake

chef Yvonne Kreck

ingredients

Crust

1 packet (1/3 box) of chocolate graham crackers, crushed
1/3 cup butter
1/4 cup sugar

Filling

5 ounces semisweet chocolate
2 8-ounce packages cream cheese, softened
1-1/4 cups sugar
2 tablespoons all-purpose flour
1 teaspoon vanilla
4 eggs
1/4 cup Mill Creek Chocolate Cabernet Sauce

directions preheat oven to 350°

For the crust, in a large bowl, combine the crushed chocolate graham crackers with the butter and sugar. In an ungreased, 9-inch springform pan, press the mixture evenly into the bottom and 1½ inches up the side of the pan. Chill in the refrigerator while preparing the filling.

For the filling, in a small heavy saucepan, melt the semisweet chocolate over low heat. In a large mixing bowl, beat the cream cheese, sugar, flour and vanilla with an electric mixer set on medium speed, until the batter is smooth. Switch the mixer speed to low, and slowly add the melted chocolate. Beat on low until combined. Add the eggs all at once, and continue to beat on low speed just until the mixture is combined. Stir in the Chocolate Cabernet Sauce by hand.

Remove the crust-lined pan from the refrigerator and add the filling. Place the springform pan in a shallow baking pan and bake for 45-50 minutes, until the center of the filling appears set when the pan is gently shaken. A knife inserted in the center should come out clean.

Cool the cheesecake in the pan on a wire rack for 15 minutes. Using a sharp knife, loosen the crust from the sides of the pan, and let the cake cool for 30 minutes more. Remove the sides of the springform pan, and cool 1 hour longer. Cover and chill at least 4 hours before serving.

pair with mill creek left of starboard port-style wine

The Shelford House Inn

29955 river road, cloverdale, ca 95425
800-833-6479

www.shelford.com

The combination of peanut butter and chocolate made Reese's Peanut Butter Cups famous. Shelford House innkeeper Anna Smith takes this glorious combination to loftier heights in her biscotti, which she often puts out for guests returning from a day of wine tasting or an evening out. **Makes 5 dozen biscotti.**

desserts & sweets

peanut butter & chocolate
biscotti

chef Anna Smith, Innkeeper

ingredients

10 tablespoons unsalted butter
2-½ cups all-purpose flour
2-¾ teaspoons baking powder
½ teaspoon salt
3 large eggs
1-¼ cups sugar
2 teaspoons pure vanilla extract
½ cup smooth, natural peanut butter, room temperature
1-¼ cups dry-roasted peanuts
1-¼ cups dark chocolate, chopped

directions preheat oven to 350°

Line 3 baking sheets with parchment paper, and position the racks in the middle of the oven.

Melt the butter over medium heat, swirling the pan occasionally. Continue to heat until the butter browns and gives off a nutty aroma, about 5 minutes. Allow to cool slightly.

In a large bowl, whisk the flour, baking powder and salt, and set aside.

Using an electric mixer, beat the eggs in a medium-sized bowl until they're light and pale yellow, about 2 minutes. Gradually add the sugar while beating, then slowly add the browned butter and vanilla until all the ingredients are evenly mixed, about 30 seconds more.

Add the peanut butter and mix slowly. Add the dry ingredients to the wet ingredients in 2 additions, mixing just until absorbed. Fold in the peanuts and chocolate pieces.

Divide the dough evenly into thirds and put each portion in the center of the prepared baking sheets. With slightly wet hands, shape the dough into logs about 2 inches wide and 15 inches long. Bake each log until the dough is set and the cookies brown around the edges, 25-30 minutes. Rotate the baking sheets halfway through the cooking time.

Allow the logs to cool on the baking sheets for about 10 minutes.

Lower the oven temperature to 325°. Carefully transfer the logs to a cutting board and cut the logs crosswise into ½-inch-thick cookies, using a sharp serrated knife held at a 45° angle. Place the cookies, cut side down, on the baking sheets, and bake until crisp, about 8 minutes. Flip the cookies over and bake them until golden brown, about 8 minutes more.

Cool the biscotti on the baking sheets, then serve. They keep well in an air-tight container.

pair with port or any other red dessert wine

Truett Hurst Winery

5610 dry creek road, healdsburg, ca 95448
707-433-9545

www.truetthurst.com

Wendy De Meulenaere bakes a mean flourless chocolate cake, and you can, too, with her recipe. It's a great time-saver, as it can be prepared and refrigerated a few days before serving. Optionally, add a dollop of unsweetened whipped cream on each slice. **Serves 12-16**

desserts & sweets

wendy's flourless
chocolate cake

chef Wendy De Meulenaere

ingredients

11 ounces 62% semisweet chocolate or other high-quality
semisweet or bittersweet chocolate, coarsely chopped
7 ounces unsalted butter
5 large eggs
1 cup granulated sugar
unsweetened whipped cream (optional)

directions preheat oven to 350°

Position the rack in the center of the oven. Butter a 9- by 2-inch round cake pan and line the bottom with a round of parchment paper.

Set a large bowl over a pan of simmering water to create a double boiler. Put the chocolate and the butter in the bowl to melt, whisking occasionally (chocolate burns easily).

In another bowl, whisk together the eggs and sugar. Let the butter/chocolate mixture cool a little, and whisk it into the egg/sugar mixture.

Pour the batter into the buttered pan. Place it in a larger baking pan, and pour warm water into the large pan to reach 1/3 of the way up the sides of the cake pan.

Cover both pans tightly with a sheet of foil and carefully place in the oven. (You can also pour the warm water into the larger pan after you place it on the rack to avoid spillage.)

Bake the cake for 1 hour and 15 minutes, until it appears to have set and your finger comes away clean when you touch the center. Remove the cake from the water bath and let it cool completely. Invert the pan onto a plate and peel off the parchment paper. Serve in thin slices with the whipped cream.

recipe index by winery and lodging

the wineries

recipe index by winery and lodging

the wineries continued

recipe index by winery and lodging

the wineries continued

recipe index by winery and lodging
the lodgings

new look, new name, another milestone!

WINE ROAD
NORTHERN SONOMA COUNTY

This year, the Russian River Wine Road unveiled a new logo and name — Wine Road Northern Sonoma County — coinciding with the announcement that the 150th vintner joined the organization, making Wine Road Northern Sonoma County one of the largest winery associations in Sonoma County.

The Wine Road promotes Northern Sonoma County as a world-class wine producing region and a top travel destination for foodies, oenophiles and outdoor enthusiasts alike. "This is a monumental milestone, considering the association was founded with only nine members more than three decades ago. We look forward to continued growth and are excited to unveil our new look and name," says Beth Costa, Executive Director of the Wine Road.

The Wine Road represents vintners from the Russian River, Alexander and Dry Creek valleys, and is home to three celebrated wine events throughout the year — "Winter Wineland" in January, "Barrel Tasting" in March and "A Wine & Food Affair" in November.

Combined, these events offer guests the opportunity to visit the wineries, meet the vintners and sample their wines along with the finest in local cuisine. Each event attracts wine collectors, connoisseurs, and food and wine enthusiasts from around the globe, while highlighting the region's wine country lifestyle, including its hospitable locals, renowned wine producers, and scenic beauty.

To further promote its members and the region, the Wine Road launched a redesigned web site, www.wineroad.com, offering visitors a comprehensive resource for travel to Northern Sonoma County. The new site provides users with an expansive overview of the region, along with detailed information on its winery members, including new wine releases and winery events. Planning a visit to the area is much easier now, with printable maps, travelogues and an alphabetical list of wineries, lodgings and lodging specials. Visitors can easily access information on its winery members, lodging affiliates, events, activities, transportation, shopping, dining and more.

The Wine Road is an association of nearly 160 wineries and 50 lodgings throughout the Alexander, Dry Creek and Russian River valleys in Northern Sonoma County, a stunning landscape dotted with wineries and picturesque towns. The grandeur of the Pacific Ocean and towering redwoods leads visitors inland along quiet country roads, just one hour north of San Francisco. And … there is always something going on along the Wine Road, with year-round winery events, exciting new releases of vintages, and much more. For more information or to request a free map, call 800-723-6336 or email info@wineroad.com. Please visit the web site at www.wineroad.com.

events

Annual **Wine Road Northern Sonoma County** Events

Winter Wineland
January - Martin Luther King Jr Birthday Weekend

A great opportunity to meet winemakers and taste limited-production wines. Several participating wineries are not generally open to the public. Make it a three-day weekend of wine tasting, winemaker chats, winery tours and seminars.

Tickets are available in advance, online: $40 for the weekend, $30 for Sunday only, and $10 for designated drivers. Once online tickets sales end, prices at the door are $50 weekend, $40 Sunday only and $10 designated drivers. Online tickets go on sale the previous November at www.wineroad.com.

Barrel Tasting
March - First two weekends

A chance to sample wines from the barrel and talk with winemakers. It's also a special opportunity to purchase "futures," often at a discount. Come back to the winery after the wine is bottled (typically 12-16 months later) and pick up your purchase. The production of many member wineries is so limited that buying futures is your only chance to purchase the wine you like.

Tickets are available in advance, online: $20 per person, per weekend, and $10 for designated drivers, per weekend. Once online tickets sales end, prices at the door are $30 per person, per weekend; designated drivers will remain $10 per weekend.

A Wine & Food Affair
November - The first full weekend

Our premier event: A full weekend of wine and food pairings, complete with the current volume of "Tasting Along the Wine Road" cookbook and event logo glass. All participating wineries will have a recipe for a favorite dish in the cookbook, which they will prepare both days for you to sample, paired with the perfect wine. Many Wine Road lodgings also provide recipes for inclusion in the cookbook.

Tickets are available in advance, online: $60 for the weekend, $40 for Sunday only and $25 for designated drivers. Online tickets go on sale the previous September at www.wineroad.com. (Once online tickets sales end, the price at the door is the same, but will not include the cookbook).

For details on these annual events and other wine
country festivities sponsored by our members, visit
www.wineroad.com

our AVAs (american viticultural areas)

Alexander Valley

Total acres: 32,536 • Vineyard acres: 15,000 • Number of wineries: 49, growing 23 grape varieties

This valley is named for the 19th-century pioneer Cyrus Alexander, explorer of Northern Sonoma County and resident of the area. Alexander Valley flanks the Russian River from Cloverdale to Healdsburg. Along the heavily graveled benchlands, one finds world-class Cabernet Sauvignon grapes. Considered one of the most diverse grapegrowing regions in California, the valley is also planted to Chardonnay, Zinfandel, Merlot, Sauvignon Blanc and other varieties, which prosper on the long, undulating valley floor and hillsides.

Forty years ago, prunes and walnuts reigned supreme in the Alexander Valley, and the flatlands were dotted with bovine herds. Today, the lowlands produce Chardonnays that achieve a rich and flavorful ripeness. The warmer northern end of the valley favors Cabernet Sauvignon, Zinfandel, Merlot and newcomers like French Syrah and Italian Sangiovese. Vineyards that scale the hillsides surrounding the valley floor provide grapes with deep and complex flavors. Hunt around and you can also still find some of the juiciest, most succulent prunes you've ever tasted.

Dry Creek Valley

Total acres: 78,387 • Vineyard acres: 10,000 • Number of wineries: 81, growing 26 grape varieties

In many ways, Dry Creek Valley is quintessentially Sonoma County, where warm days are tempered by morning fog from the Pacific Ocean, and food-friendly varieties such as Sauvignon Blanc and Zinfandel boldly emerge, both on the narrow valley floor and the wooded hillsides above.

Originally planted by French immigrants in 1870, Dry Creek Valley attracted Italian immigrants who discovered the geography was reminiscent of their native Tuscany and Piedmont. They planted Petite Sirah, Zinfandel and Carignane to produce hearty red wines. Today, the leading varieties, after Zinfandel, include Cabernet Sauvignon, Sauvignon Blanc and Merlot. The severe, stone-strewn soils are ideal for concentrated fruit and flavor characteristics, creating wines that are truly representative of the land.

The aptly named Rockpile AVA emerged from the northern tip of Dry Creek Valley in 2002. Known for its warm and sunny climate, and named for its rough and unrelenting terrain, this area cultivates rich Zinfandel, Petite Sirah, Syrah and Cabernet Sauvignon.

Russian River Valley

Total acres: 126,600 • Vineyard acres: 10,000 • Number of wineries: 130, growing 30 grape varieties

What makes Russian River Valley stand out is its climate. This low-lying flat plain extends south and west of Healdsburg as it winds its way along the Russian River and descends to meet the Pacific at Jenner, then makes it way toward the Golden Gate Bridge, ending about 55 miles north of this landmark. This area thrives from the coastal influences of the Pacific Ocean, which makes it an exceptional place for growing cool-climate grapes like Pinot Noir, Chardonnay as well as sparkling wine grapes.

The Russian River Valley is so expansive that it has two smaller appellations within it: Green Valley of Sonoma County and Chalk Hill. Green Valley is one of the smallest appellations in the county, nestled in the southwest corner of the Russian River Valley. This area is greatly affected by the cooling coastal elements, which benefit the cool-climate grapes that flourish in these conditions. Chalk Hill, named for the volcanic soil that makes up the area, is a unique little gem known for its outstanding wines. By being situated in the northwest corner of Russian River Valley, it has warmer temperatures that allow Merlot and Cabernet Sauvignon to thrive.

Russian River Valley Chardonnays are exceptional, slightly more lean and refined than those of Alexander Valley, yet the fruit is still developed enough to sustain months in oak barrels, creating depth and complexity. Pinot Noir brought this area international acclaim. Whereas most red wines focus on flavor, Pinot Noir is about an alluring, sensual, velvety mouth-feel. It is a textural delight that can only be found where morning fog turns to warm afternoons, so that grape maturity is achieved without loss of depth and suppleness.

regional information

our AVAs (american viticultural areas)

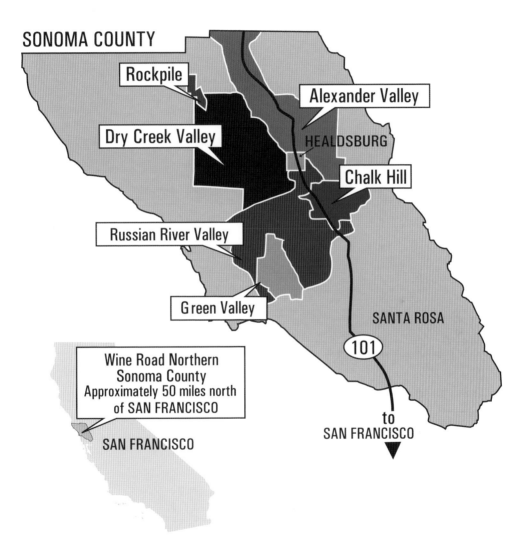

SONOMA COUNTY

Rockpile

Alexander Valley

Dry Creek Valley

HEALDSBURG

Chalk Hill

Russian River Valley

Green Valley

SANTA ROSA

101

Wine Road Northern
Sonoma County
Approximately 50 miles north
of SAN FRANCISCO

SAN FRANCISCO

to
SAN FRANCISCO

Wine Road Northern Sonoma County

another $30,000 donation

In April 2009, Wine Road Executive Director Beth Costa and President Nancy Woods presented the Redwood Empire Food Bank with a portion of the proceeds from this year's 31st annual Barrel Tasting. More than 100 wineries located in the Dry Creek, Russian River and Alexander valleys threw open their cellar doors to celebrate the 2009 Barrel Tasting, and during the two weekends, raised an impressive $30,000 for the Food Bank.

The Food Bank serves 60,000 people in Sonoma, Mendocino, Lake, Humboldt and Del Norte counties each month, including children, seniors and working families.

"The Wine Road is proud to support the Redwood Empire Food Bank and in turn, those in need in the community," Costa says. "We are so proud of the fact that our contributions to this organization over the last five years now total more than $100,000. Our members can truly be proud."

Lee Bickley from REFP, Beth Costa and Nancy Woods from Wine Road and David Goodman from REFB.

This year's $30,000 donation was a combination of $22,000 from the Wine Road, $6,500 from ARES, the ticketing agency that sold Barrel Tasting tickets online, and guests who made online donations totaling $1,500 at the time they ordered tickets.

REDWOOD EMPIRE
FOOD BANK

In addition to the donation from Barrel Tasting, $1.00 for every ticket sold for A Wine & Food Affair is donated to the Redwood Empire Food Bank. For more information about REFB or to make a donation, please log onto www.refb.com.

it's good to be green...

The winds of change are blowing along the Wine Road...

We're looking at our surroundings and finding ways that we can make sure our environmental impact is as minimal as possible.

Starting in 2008, the Wine Road began reducing plastic waste by providing event attendees with Calistoga drinking water from refillable, multi-gallon containers. Guests dispense water directly into their event wine glasses, instead of drinking from individual plastic bottles.

After the events, these water containers are returned to the Calistoga Beverage Co., to be refilled and used time and time again.

To reduce paper consumption, Wine Road no longer mails event invitations to the thousands of people on our mailing list. Instead, we reach out to our guests via online invitations. We count on everyone to help us spread the word about our events and happenings, and have added "share" buttons to our web site so that you can easily e-mail all the news to friends and family.

In addition, we no longer print and mail tickets; guests simply order online and print e-tickets at home. Detailed event programs are available in PDF format on our web site.

Rather than mailing newsletters, we keep visitors updated via online sources; follow us on Facebook and Twitter. Sign up for our e-mail news, which we send out monthly, with lodging specials and event information from our members.